TRANSFORMING EDUCATION THROUGH TOTAL QUALITY MANAGEMENT: A PRACTITIONER'S GUIDE

Franklin P. Schargel
Quality Coordinator
George Westinghouse Vocational and
Technical High School
Brooklyn, New York

EYE ON EDUCATION
P.O. BOX 388
PRINCETON JUNCTION, NJ 08550
(609) 799-9188
(609) 799-3698 fax

Editorial and production services provided by Richard H. Adin Freelance
Editorial Services, 96 Rabbit Run Road, Clintondale, NY 12515 (914-883-
5884)
Graphic art provided by Nightshift Computer Graphics, 155 Howard Street,
Dumont, NJ 07628

ISBN 1-883001-07-2

Library of Congress Cataloging-in-Publication Data

Schargel, Franklin P.
    Transforming education through total quality management: a
practitioner's guide / Franklin P. Schargel
        p.   cm.
    Includes bibliographical references.
    ISBN 1-883001-07-2
    1. School management and organization—United States. 2. Total
quality management—United States. I. Title.
LB2805.S32 1994
371.2'00973—dc20   93-46527
                                                        CIP

Mr. Franklin P. Schargel
Quality Coordinator
George Westinghouse Vocational
  and Technical High School
105 Johnson Street
Brooklyn, New York 11201

Dear Mr. Schargel:

Congratulations for the success you have achieved in the use of Total Management Techniques at George Westinghouse Vocational and Technical High School.

The Department of Labor concurs that high quality management can be an important tool in enhancing many organizations. In addition, along with the Department of Education, we have strongly supported business-educational linkages combined with strong Tech Prep programs which include work-based learning.

I sincerely hope that all who endeavor to improve schools in the way George Westinghouse High School has done will have the types of outstanding results in the areas of dropout reduction, post-secondary attendance, parental involvement and good press which you have reported.

Keep up the good work!

Sincerely,

Robert B. Reich

In Memorium

Dr. William Edwards Deming
October 14, 1900–December 20, 1993
The Father of Quality

DEDICATION

This book is dedicated to the over
two million teachers who work in 83,000 public
schools in 15,000 school districts,

and to

my parents, Aaron and Pauline,
my wife, Sandy,
and my children, David and Howard,
who taught me the true meaning of quality before I
ever heard about TQM.

Alice said to the Cheshire Cat,
"Would you tell me, please, which way I
ought to go from here?"
"That depends a good deal on where you want
to get to,"
said the Cat.
"I don't much care where," said Alice.
"Then it doesn't matter which way you go,"
said the Cat.

Alice's Adventures in Wonderland
by
Lewis Carroll

ACKNOWLEDGEMENTS

While the author will take the credit (and the blame) for being the inspiration and driving force of what is taking place at George Westinghouse, Total Quality Education could not have taken place without the bold, dynamic, and couragous leadership of my friend and colleague, Lewis A. Rappaport.

I want to thank my son, Howard Mark Schargel for his illustrations and charts. Edward W. Bales, Mark Gavoor, and Jeanne Benecke contributed with their suggestions and writing.

I am indebted to a number of people who served as teachers and mentors. Frank Caplan of Quality Sciences Consultants, Inc, Ed Bayles of Motorola, Larrae Rocheleau, the Superintendent of Mount Edgecombe High School, Sitka Alaska, the late Robert Cox and Steve Michaels of National Westminster Bank USA, Larry Schiff, Jim Courage, and "Woody" Bliss of IBM, Diane Ritter of GOAL/QPC, Mel Silberberg of the National Education Quality Initiative, and Wayne Mize of the Ricoh Corporation. To Alan Randell, who serves as the Social Studies Coordinator at Westinghouse, I owe an enormous debt of gratitude. I could not have done what I did in Total Quality unless he helped make my office run. To Robert W. Ohlerking, who frequently listened to my ideas and offered advice and frequently heard my gripes, I owe a great debt.

As for the unselfish efforts of the members of the Westinghouse Quality Steering Committee who gave of their time, talents, and energy not enough can be said.

Westinghouse Quality Steering Committee

Bob Johnson	English
Mark Potecha	Special Education
Dulcie Reid	Social Studies
Tom Omerza	TV Studio
Ken Stanton	English
Brenda Giammanco	Secretary
Caroline Albert	English
Ed Falcone	Trade and Tech
Linda Mc Lean	Guidance
Gerald Jay	Dental
Jean Benecke	Math
Robert Serkey	Math/Science
Alan Randell	Social Studies
Jim Reilly	Trade and Tech
Michael Graff	Social Studies
Jean Claude Brizard	Science
Roy Garrett	Physical Education
Kent Schleicher	Social Studies
Alison Bassell	English
Brad Rose	Woodworking
Derek Pearl	Jewelry Department
Arthur Kutcher	Jewelry Department
Harvey Krasnow	Administration
Julia Gandhi	Special Education
Vera Zimmerman	Special Education
Michael Graff	United Federation of Teachers

Franklin P. Schargel
December, 1993

As Assistant Principal and Quality Coordinator, Franklin Schargel has been the driving force behind the transformation of George Westinghouse Vocational and Technical High School. Mr. Schargel is an internationally recognized speaker and author. His articles have appeared in numerous journals, including *Quality Progress* and *Quality Digest*. He has presented at conferences sponsored by AASA, GOAL/QPC, and ASQC.

Table of Contents

3: GETTING TO KNOW GEORGE WESTINGHOUSE VOC/TECH HIGH SCHOOL

4: GETTING STARTED STRATEGIES

5: GETTING THE STAFF INVOLVED

FOREWORD

The role of the business community is to create wealth which generates the tax base to pay for the public sector. Business is, therefore, the final customer of the education system. Corporations are dependent on public and private schools to develop workers who can add value to the work place through skills learned in school. There is general agreement among world leaders that the future economic wealth of society is dependent upon the education of the young.

This world of work has changed dramatically from the traditional industrial model (upon which the design of the present education system was based) to the information model. In the new model, knowledge is the strategic resource, and the driving force is the human mind. The work force must have life-long learning skills in order to cope with the rapid and continuous changes currently taking place in global societies. In addition, writing, verbal-communication, and interpersonal skills are an absolute necessity for team-driven problem solving. Complex thinking skills are necessary to innovate and create new ways of doing things. Self-esteem is indispensable in order to tap the potential of every member of the enterprise. Self-esteem should lead to treating every other person with integrity and respect so that the maximum potential of each member of society can be realized. All of these skills must be learned while young people are in school.

The skills I have just described are learned through experience, involvement in a system where students are the people responsible for their own learning. At George Westinghouse Vocational and Technical High School in Brooklyn, New York, a model is developing which creates learning of skills through role modelling and high expectations for all. At Westinghouse, this model of learning is driven through their total quality education process.

A basic management practice of any Total Quality Management model requires input from all those who are involved in the work being done. At Westinghouse the principal and quality coordinator have an advisory committee of students, parents and staff which supplies suggestions on ways to improve both teaching and learning in the school. Team teaching and team learning are integrated throughout the student's day. A focus on performance rather than time is the basic philosophy. This can be seen in the integration of several periods assembled together so the students can learn in two to three hour blocks rather than 42-minute disconnected periods of time. Students are expected to provide solutions to problems rather than management providing solutions to those who are doing the work.

The results, as you will see by reading this book, are amazing. Students are having fun learning. Teachers are facilitating learning and are extremely enthusiastic about being involved in the process. The model of Westinghouse as described in this book prevents those in education and business who would resist change from saying it can't be done. It is being done and this book describes how.

In our corporation, we have moved from a focus on a specific quality goal to a process of continuous improvement. However, continuous improvement requires continuous change and continuous change requires continuous learning.

Westinghouse is not only a model of continuous learning, but is under going this process as an organization in itself. This book describes what has been learned so far. As will be shown, the process of change is messy and painful. Many more lessons are yet to be learned. However, Westinghouse is well on its way to becoming a total quality education organization.

Edward W. Bales
Director of Education-External Systems
Motorola Incorporated

INTRODUCTION

WHY WE NEED TOTAL QUALITY MANAGEMENT IN EDUCATION

The end of the second World War left the United States not only the world's military leader, but its economic leader as well. The Allies suffered enormously, both in their industrial capacity and with their workforce as well. Beginning with the Marshall Plan (1948) and, to a lesser degree, Point Four, United States manufacturers were able to sell at home and to the rest of the world all that they were capable of producing. Quantity, not quality became the operational philosophy. If the consumer didn't like the product, he didn't have to buy it! There wasn't a need for the businessperson to concentrate on rebuilding America's factories or to concentrate on product improvement. The United States was able to outproduce and outsell their global competitors, because there weren't any.

American manufacturers became complacent and arrogant. Perhaps that arrogance was best expressed by Charles Wilson, the Chief Executive Officer of General Motors who stated, "What is good for General Motors is good for America." Due to the lack of competitive goods from foreign countries, everything produced was sold. Businesspeople were far more concerned with short-term financial returns than long-term research. American manufacturers became recognized for products that didn't work or broke down. What industrialists failed to recognize was that producing a defective product, which had to be repaired or replaced, was just as expensive as producing a satisfactory product. Rework and repair became a component in the cost of production of acceptable products.

If the products were inexpensive, the consumer threw them out. If the products were expensive, the consumer had them repaired. What was not figured into the cost of the product was consumer dissatisfaction. How do you measure consumer dissatisfaction? Dissatisfied consumers tell many other people of their dissatisfaction.

Between 1945 and 1949 Japanese products were considered to be of inferior quality and poorly made. The label "Made in Japan" or "Made in Occupied Japan" indicated shoddiness. American experts were called in. One of the first was Dr. W. Edwards Deming. In 1949, Dr. Deming proposed to a group of Japanese industrialists that in rebuilding their industries they should make a nationwide assault on inferior quality. The result is popularly called Total Quality Management. Today, in Japan, Deming is adored. His pictures hang in the headquarters of some of Japan's leading corporations alongside of the pictures of the Chief Executive Officer and founder. The top Japanese award for quality is named after an American, the Deming Prize.

In the 1950's American manufacturers disregarded the rebirth of European and Japanese industrial production. A "no one can touch us attitude" permeated throughout American industry. By the 1960's it was difficult to ignore losses of market share to Volkswagon and Seiko. By 1960, the Japanese were the world's biggest ship builders. The 1970's saw the erosion, and ultimately the loss, of American industries like radio, television, and watches. The concept that the Japanese were best able to copy Western processes proved false. The Japanese became pre-eminent in automobiles, steel, textiles, televisions, watches, cameras, and binoculars, traditionally considered Western manufacturing fields. It was the Japanese who developed the new technological industries of fax machines, portable electronics like the "Walkman," and robotronics. America had the technology first, but failed to implement it.

The Japanese have been able to succeed for a number of reasons:

- ◆ The commitment to Total Quality Management has become a part of their culture.
- ◆ Their ability to tap their human resources.
- ◆ The hesitancy of the American business community to commit to Total Quality Management.
- ◆ Their ability to depend on a competent technologically-trained high school and college graduate.

Americans began to find excuses why the world was flocking to Japanese products. It was said that the Japanese were using low cost labor, that they were dumping, that they had made savings because they weren't putting money into military expenditures, etc. While all of these factors were true to some degree, no one accused the Japanese of producing a superior product. It is indeed ironic that today Americans, and people in the rest of the industrialized world, purchase superior quality goods from Japan while *American-made goods are perceived as being poorly made and of inferior quality.*

In the 1980's a number of American companies became very concerned. By 1982 Xerox had lost 50% of its market share *in a product they had invented!* David Kearns, then Chief Executive Officer, was worried when he found Japanese photocopier companies selling photocopiers for less than it cost Xerox to manufacture! He saw the possibility of Xerox going out of business within 10 years unless there was a dramatic change in the way Xerox conducted its business. Kearns decided that the best way to recoup market share for Xerox was to duplicate the Japanese emphasis on quality manufacturing and service.

Today the American business community feels that it can re-emerge as the pre-eminent world industrial leader by re-establishing the high quality of its products and services. In these efforts, millions of dollars have been invested by companies, large and small, to give employees training in quality techniques. In 1987, America created the Malcolm Baldridge National Quality Award to "recognize United States companies that excel in quality management and quality achievement." Yet, even today, the name "Deming" is virtually unknown to most Americans. His name cannot be found in any of America's encyclopedias.

Can America succeed? Japan with its extremely limited natural resources has had to focus on its human resources. Conversely, America, since World War II, with its seemingly limitless natural resources and a work force fueled with a constant flow of immigrants, has failed to concentrate on either productivity or worker quality.

The "Scientific Management" techniques developed by Frederick Winslow Taylor were used through most of this century in the United States and Europe. It demanded workers that obeyed rather than thought. The techniques were dependent on a college educated or on-the-job trained management team. A compliant, complacent labor force was willing to take orders and mindlessly fill them. People who failed to complete elementary or secondary schools were easily absorbed into the rapidly expanding unskilled or semi-skilled work force.

The Taylor model will not work in the last decade of the 20th century nor in the 21st century. Workers must be prepared to meet the technological challenges posed by automation and robotronics. If workers are viewed merely as expendable or as another "tool" in the production process, then United States industrial production will continue to falter.

America's public schools have been largely ignored and left out of the paradigm shift to Total Quality Management. Possibly, they have been ignored because they have been such a disaster. Everyone knows that America's public schools are not working the way they should. America's schools are failing to deliver the product that they have been designed to produce—an educated individual. The schools have failed to produce graduates capable of reading, writing, doing math, thinking, coming on time, and working cooperatively. If America's schools are unable to produce its products, how then can America's industries produce theirs? Imagine a business where one-third of the product is scrapped before it ever reaches the end of the production process. Imagine a business where the product reaching the end of the production process fails to satisfy the customer and is incapable of doing what it is required of it. That is a description of the American public school system of today.

The schools, once envisioned as the cauldron of the melting pot, producing from the masses future military leaders, engineers, scientists, doctors, presidents, and industrial leaders, are facing major problems.

The problems of our schools are well-known:

◆ Test scores are declining;
◆ The dropout rate has reached pandemic levels, particularly among poor and minority students;
◆ Students with high school diplomas are unable to read, comprehend or do mathematical problems, think or work in teams at levels required in the new workplace;
◆ Many high school and college graduates have inadequate basic skills;
◆ Nationally there is insufficient support for our schools and our teachers;
◆ There is a shortage of people trained in science and technology;
◆ The nation's colleges and industries are burdened with giving remediation courses— teaching what should have been learned in high school.

How can America hope to compete in the world's marketplace when:

◆ More than half of City University of New York students fails to graduate within six years. A mere 15% achieve a bachelor's degree in four years.

◆ Twenty-one million adults in the US cannot read even at the fourth-grade level.

◆ Eighty percent of the job applicants failed Motorola's ninth-grade-level English comprehension test.

◆ Even though the Chrysler Corporation rewrote its training manuals to an eighth grade reading level, more than 25% of present employees failed.

◆ The National Assessment for Progress found that only 1 in 5 people between the ages of 21 and 25 could read a bus timetable or draft a letter asking for a job in a supermarket.

◆ One-fourth of adults do not know if the sun goes around the earth or vice versa.

◆ In 1987 the New York Telephone Company had to screen 57,000 applicants to find 2000 with the skills to become entry-level operators and repair technicians.

◆ One-fourth of all students who start in American high schools fails to graduate with their class—30% drop out; the percentages for Blacks and Hispanics are higher.

◆ Jonathan Kozol, in his book, *Illiterate America,* states there are 60 million Americans who cannot read a classified employment advertisement.

◆ According to *Time Magazine* (June 1987) there are a million students who graduate from high school each year who are unable to read.

◆ After 6 years less than one-half of students at four year colleges have earned a degree. Graduation rates at community colleges are even lower. Fewer than one-third of those entering State University of New York Community Colleges gets a degree at the end of 2 years.

Society has dramatically changed since the time when America's schools were seen as the world's finest—able to absorb tens of thousands of non-English speaking immigrants, assimilate them and turn them into productive members of the world's fastest-growing and most-productive economic system.

Today many young people enter the job market unprepared, and American business is increasingly unable to find skilled workers. Does it make sense for the American business community to hire the best of the worst? The success of America's business community is inexorably tied to the American public school system. The K–12 education system has students for 13 years, while the workplace will have them for between 40 and 50 years. Therefore, if America's schools are incapable of producing graduates capable of reading, writing, doing math, and thinking, then America's businesses are doomed to fail. Without a well-trained work force, American business cannot expect to be competitive in the complex world marketplace. Currently, the American business community spends $25 billion a year training entry-level employees skills that should have been acquired in the nation's high schools and colleges. As John Akers, former Chairman of IBM stated, "Education isn't just a social concern, it's a major economic issue. If our students can't compete today, how will our companies compete tomorrow?"

The competitiveness of the global economy makes change a foregone conclusion. Faced with the rising competition in the global marketplace and the declining achievement levels of public school students, there is a demand for the redesign of the schools. Some proposals, while radical, fail to deal with the fundamental or root problems of the schools. The suggestions take many forms (*e.g.,* Black schools for Black male youths; School Based Management; Shared Decision Making; extending of the school year; lengthening the school day; privatization of the schools). These recommendations strike at the symptoms of the challenges rather than at the root causes. Many of the solutions to the myriad of educational problems provide a "quick fix," bandaid approach to an educational system which is hemorrhaging. They tamper with a process which must be systemically changed. America's love affair with the quick fix has obscured the complexities involved with the overhauling of a system that handles forty million individual students. Many of education's problems did not develop overnight; we cannot expect to solve them overnight. What is needed is a process designed to identify the root causes of school failure and remove them.

Traditionally, we blame our problems on people. The parents blame the schools; the schools blame the parents and the students. Everyone blames a number of external forces: television, violence in the home and in the media, the demise of the nuclear family, drugs, and the lack of funding. The lament goes, "If only we had more interested parents . . ." or "if only we had better students. . . ." This sounds like the proverbial carpenter blaming his tools for the defective building he's constructing. Now is not the time to attempt to fix the blame; rather we must fix the process running the system system. We must come to realize that everyone has a stake in the future of our nation's children.

Yet, for all of these proposed changes, there are a myriad of new challenges. If some people concluded in 1992 that the American workforce is lazy, illiterate, and uninspired by the work ethic, imagine what they will conclude as America's current school population enters the workforce. The current school population has a growing number of children who:

- have been exposed prenatally to drugs or alcohol
- are homeless
- are abused and neglected
- have been exposed to violence in school and
  within the family
- are affected with the H.I.V. virus
- live in single parent homes
- are parents themselves.

In addition, the percentage of minority students is increasing significantly. These students traditionally have the nation's highest dropout and pregnancy rates. Today, almost 30% of students in public schools, about 12 million, are minorities. The figure could reach 40% by the year 2000, when minorities are expected to account for 60% of the nation's population growth.

It is expected that by the year 2080 today's minority workforce will be the *majority* workforce.

Almost half of all young women who drop out of school do so because of pregnancy. More than half the African-American children in this country live with a single never-married parent.

Jack A. MacAllister, Chairman and CEO, USWEST,Inc., and co-chair of Business Partnership of the Education Commission of the States, has stated, "At the rate we're going America's labor force will simply not have the skills necessary to keep us competitive in the global market place by the year 2000. . . . The quality of our schools determines the quality of our workforce. Far too many young people leave school untrained and unskilled. Some leave school unprepared because that's the way they went in. . . . The only thing more expensive than education, a wise man observed, is ignorance."

It is vital to the United States economy that the greatest number of jobs becoming available will be in high skill occupations requiring significant thinking skills. It is predicted that there will be an insufficient number of workers capable of utilizing new business technologies in the year 2000.

At the same time, schools are being forced to downsize, taking cuts in resources and revenue. But the answer to America's public school system challenge is not merely to throw money at the system, as we did in the 1960's. We should provide the means to change and coalesce the forces interested in saving of the system.

The introduction of the quality concept should be implanted early in American society, in the schools, and filter up to the workplace. If the concept of quality is to work it must filter up from the schools, not trickle down from industry. The Total Quality Management movement must move concurrently into utilizing TQM techniques and tools in schools as well as industry. America will never rise again without an improved school system. Total Quality Education (TQE) has the ability to lead American education into the 21st century.

At George Westinghouse Vocational and Technical High School, we believe that the United States cannot continue to be a world class power if it does not have world class schools. In 1988, we began implementing Total Quality Management techniques in changing our instructional process. The challenge was to see if these techniques developed by Deming, *et. al.,* would work in education. We felt that the Total Quality Management principles that help Japanese and American corporations compete globally are the same principles that can be applied to improve the public schools and the education delivery system. We believe that students, parents, and staff, given the proper motivation, training, and tools are best able to deal with the challenges facing the schools.

If Total Quality Management could be successfully used in an inner-city school like Westinghouse, then it can be used in schools throughout the country. If quality principles can lead American industry out of economic crisis, imagine what Total Quality Education might do for American education. We know that we must restructure the system, redirect it and change the way we manage it. We must shift the way we view education. The system must be redirected from serving the owners of the system to serving its customers. We must encourage this change by organizing the forces interested in the rebuilding of the system.

This book is intended to serve as a handbook to show how one school has been applying these techniques. It is designed to provide a beginning—a beginning that almost any school, teacher or parent can undertake today, using existing resources. We believe that by using Westinghouse as a model the reader can learn some of the things to avoid. We are not the only model! We are among the growing number of schools who are breaking the ice so that others may follow. This book is written with the hope that other schools can avoid the pitfalls we faced and shorten their learning curve.

1

WHAT IS TOTAL QUALITY EDUCATION?

How have the Japanese been able to become the envy of the industrialized world? How have they been able to leap past the French, Russians and English to share the title of economic superpower with the United States? How is a country with virtually no natural resources, able to produce so many superb products?

The Japanese Quality Movement has been evolving since the 1920's. In 1950, the Japanese began to embrace the philosophies of Dr. W. Edwards Deming, Joseph M. Juran, and several other theorists. Over the past forty years, this philosophy has become ingrained into the Japanese culture. The Japanese refer to this technique as "Total Quality Control" or TQC. In the United States, the most commonly used phrase is TQM or Total Quality Management. Some of the quality "gurus," Dr. Deming among them, object to using this phrase.

In order to avoid confusing the reader with the different names for this technique we will use Total Quality Management. We call the educational application "Total Quality Education (TQE)."

Total Quality Management is not a trick or a gimmick. It is a process which involves a strategy requiring a different way of doing things. We, at Westinghouse, have defined Total Quality Education this way:

Total Quality Education is a process
which involves focussing on:
meeting and exceeding customer expectations, continuous improvement, sharing responsibilities with employees
and
reducing scrap and rework.

MEETING AND EXCEEDING CUSTOMER EXPECTATIONS

The most dramatic aspect of the paradigm shift is the focus on meeting and exceeding customer expectations. America's business strategy for many years (between the 1950's to about 1980) was to ignore its customers' desire for quality and low cost. It didn't take long for the American consumer to find that the Japanese manufacturers would supply them with what they wanted, rather then telling them what was good for them. When the American consumer asked for an efficient, reliable, low-cost product, the Japanese manufacturers gladly filled the void that the American manufacturers wouldn't or couldn't fill.

Exceeding customer expectations means anticipating the future needs of customers, taking risks and developing products and services that customers never envisioned they would want or need. (This is what the Japanese did.) Who among us "asked for" remote control for television sets and video recorders, facsimile machines, "Post-its," or shampoo in hotel rooms?

Like the business community, school systems are composed of suppliers and customers and an end product. A customer is someone without whom a business cannot survive. Westinghouse High School's suppliers include elementary and intermediate schools, parents, and the community. In education, some of our internal customers are our employees, our students, and their parents. Our external customers include colleges and universities, businesses, the military, and the community at large. It is important for schools to work with both the suppliers and customers in order to produce a product which meets the expectations of the customers.

CONTINUOUS IMPROVEMENT

Continuous improvement means you are never done. Once on the path in pursuit of quality, the process must be continuously improved by altering, adding to, subtracting from, and refining.

Businesspeople who become complacent and believe that they have satisfied their customers today find that customers' expectations continue to rise. Once set in motion, the raising of the bar of customer expectations is difficult, if not impossible to stop. Ten years ago, we were satisfied if we received a sliver of soap in hotel rooms. Now if we do not get shampoo, a hair dryer, hair conditioner, mouthwash, shoe polishers, and coffee, we become upset.

Inherent in Total Quality Management is the Deming Cycle, also called the Shewart Cycle or PDCA Cycle of Plan, Do, Check, Act which, once completed, starts all over. The Shewart Cycle indicates that problem solving is never ending. One frequently hears that the Quality race is one without a finish line.

SHARING RESPONSIBILITY WITH EMPLOYEES

Quality experts believe that those closest to a problem should be involved in its solution. This is the concept of "empowerment" or, as we prefer to call it, the sharing of responsibilities, with our employees.

Teachers comprise a highly educated, dedicated, hard-working group of people who for centuries have been told how to do their job. They have been told this by the bureaucrats, administrators, politicians, parents, businesspeople, students, and college professors, many of who haven't been in a public school classroom for a generation. In spite of all of the advice classroom teachers have received, school achievement levels have not improved. We feel now is the time to ask for their assistance in reforming the instructional process.

REDUCING SCRAP AND REWORK

Industry has found that the reduction of scrap, rework, and variation adds to the bottom line. Traditionally, "quality inspectors" stood at the end of the production line inspecting for defects. This became self-defeating. It is more expensive to make a defective product than it is to make a good product because of the need to rework or scrap the product. If quality can be built into the process of manufacturing a product rather than inspected in at the end of production, enormous savings would result.

In education, we are familiar with the cycle of rework. Students who fail to master the material taught must repeat the subject. The cost of remediation is enormous. Students, teachers and parents become frustrated with repeated failure. Students frequently leave school rather than undergo this continued frustration. Industry calls this scrap. We call it dropping out.

Two other principles, not in our definition, play an important part in our quality philosophy.

1. *The process is data driven.*

Computers have given us reams and reams of information. In education, the volumes of paper are infrequently looked at and, even more rarely, used. Management should be by fact, using data taking and statistical analyses before decisions are made. Total Quality Management is driven by data. TQM uses data to design solutions rather than for record keeping purposes. Many decisions, in education are based on gut reaction or "This is the way we have always done it!" Decisions made without data, are just another opinion. As Tom Peters has stated, "What gets measured, gets done."

2. *Every educational decision should be made on the basis of how and to what extent it will add value to student learning and improve instruction.*

Each needless step wastes time, costs money, causes rework and adds to our frustration. As educators know too well, Boards of Education insist on "signing off" on everything. If a teacher wishes to take a class trip, the assistant principal must sign off. The principal and superintendent must also sign off. In New York City, trip approvals take three weeks, on average. What value has been added by these repeated sign offs?

Why should schools consider getting involved with Total Quality Management? There are a large number of reasons. The most important is that what we are doing isn't working. Educators know it isn't working and everyday we face the frustration of knowing what we are doing isn't working. The people who pay the bills know that what we are doing isn't working. They see the end product and know education isn't working. We need to find a way to make the system work. As an ancient wiseman once said, "If you try to do something and fail, you are vastly better off than if you had tried to do nothing and succeeded."

Imagine that there was a proven technique that made the job of education easier and the results better. There is! We knew when we began that Total Quality Management had worked for the Japanese and that it is working for some of America's most enlightened businesses. The question became could we customize TQM to education? Could we teach students to "Do it right the first time?" Could we reduce student recycling?

Just as America's manufacturing companies learned in the 1980's that poor quality can cost as much as 25% of their sales dollars, we in education must realize that producing a defective or unsalable product increases our costs and leads to customer dissatisfaction. David M. Gangel, Superintendent, Rappahanock County Public Schools, Sperryville, VA. said in his presentation at the Quality in Academe meeting at Lehigh University, "What costs are saved when there is less failure, retention, and remediation? It is more than monetary. The savings of self-esteem, future productivity and social institution distress could be tremendous."

When we began the process we knew that there were things that Total Quality Management would help us accomplish. We knew that TQM would:

- ◆ strengthen our organization and provide a roadmap for change and redirection;
- ◆ help us to work as teammates rather than adversaries;
- ◆ not be simply a program that would attempt to deal with one aspect of education but would be a holistic approach causing the entire school to change the way it conducted itself;

- increase the participation of everyone involved in the operation of the school (our students, faculty and staff, alumni, and the business and college community);
- lead to parents and students making suggestions to improve the educational conditions at Westinghouse;
- foster parent and student cooperation in setting quality educational standards for the school;
- cause us to become proactive rather than reactive to things that affected the school;
- impact everything that we do and the way that we do it.

We also felt that we would be able to measure our success by using the process if the following things happened:

- Higher student grades (as measured by grade point average and Scholastic Aptitude Test scores)
- Greater student involvement in school activities
- Increased admission requests
- Lower dropout rate
- Increased Parent-Teachers Association membership
- Greater involvement by faculty members in the decisionmaking process within the school
- Growing involvement by the business community in the school
- Increased recognition by the media of the school's Quality efforts.

We have been totally immersed in the process for three years. What follows is a description of what we have done. We are not finished. We never will be! The highway ahead of us is far longer than the path behind, but we know that we are on the right road! What we offer is our experience with change. We do not possess a cookbook that will apply to every school. Each school improvement process has to be customized to the needs of the school involved. We believe, however, that there are enough commonalities that everyone will be able to profit from our fledgling steps.

There were individuals who aided the Japanese in furthering their Quality movement. Each individual, whether Japanese (Shingo, Taguchi, Imai, Ishikawa) or American (Juran, Crosby, Feigenbaum) have added to the body of knowledge about quality. No individual has had a stronger impact than Dr. W. Edwards Deming and his 14 Points which have become the "10 Commandments" of the Quality movement.

DEMING'S 14 POINTS FROM "OUT OF CRISIS"

1. Create constancy of purpose for improvement of product and service.
2. Adopt the new philosophy.
3. Cease dependence on mass inspection.
4. End the practice of awarding business on price tag alone.
5. Improve constantly and forever the system of production and service.
6. Institute training.
7. Institute leadership.
8. Drive out fear.
9. Break down barriers between staff areas.
10. Eliminate slogans, exhortations, and targets for the workforce.
11. Eliminate numerical quotas.
12. Remove barriers to pride of workmanship.
13. Institute a vigorous program of education and retraining.
14. Take action to accomplish the transformation.

In implementing Total Quality Education we have, like many firms in industry, borrowed from a number of quality theorists. We do not believe that any one guru has all the answers. The foundation of our process is based on the 14 Points. Like most American companies, our Total Quality effort is an eclectic mix of the quality theories of Dr. Deming, Dr. Joseph M. Juran, Philip Crosby, and Dr. William Glasser, among others. We feel that certain points of Deming's points could not be applied to our process. We are aware that a number of schools and/or school districts have been adapting Deming to their situation. We felt that modifying our situation to suit one model was inappropriate and would not work. For example:

POINT #12 STATES "REMOVE BARRIERS TO PRIDE OF WORKMANSHIP."

Dr. Deming believes giving grades inhibit performance. In Westinghouse, we give grades for several reasons:

◆ Our grades indicate mastery of material.

Students need a way of knowing whether they have mastered the material taught. *One of the ways is a grade.* We subscribe to the belief that grades are a means of measurement and a way that students can demonstrate mastery of the material that has been taught and learned. While it may be argued that they are not an ideal method of demonstrating what students have learned, grades still should be seen as a measurement tool. Total Quality Management is not opposed to measurement. Grades call on students to demonstrate their mastery of material and not merely put in "seat time." They are one measure of what students know and to what level of proficiency they have been able to demonstrate it. Grades in Westinghouse are based on more than test scores. They are composed of several variables including attendance, punctuality, classroom performance, and outside work commitments. Until we develop other methods of rating student mastery, we will continue to use grades.

◆ Our customers demand grades.

Our students go on to college, work and the military. Our external customers want to know how our students perform. By using grades and, in the case of colleges, the Scholastic Assessment Tests, we are satisfying our customers' demands.

◆ We do not control our suppliers.

Westinghouse is composed of students from 203 junior and intermediate schools. Our suppliers—the "feeder" schools—use grades to indicate student mastery. Our parents and our students have come to expect that grades are an indication of mastery.

◆ We believe in recognition and reward.

People who work in our schools do not receive any recognition for tasks that go beyond those required by the Board of Education. In 1988, the Committee on Staff Quality Improvement at Westinghouse instituted a program to foster quality recognition at George Westinghouse and to monthly reward a staff member who has had a positive impact on students, staff, and the school community. Nominations and voting are done by staff members without the input of administrators. Senior students may also vote. Those eligible for the recognition include administrators, cafeteria workers, custodians, paraprofessionals, secretaries, security officers, teachers—anyone who works at Westinghouse High School. We place the recipient's name on the "Quality Staff Bulletin Board," award a plaque, and give a small cash award. In addition, the principal, makes the following announcement on the public address system, "Mr./Ms. _____, a teacher in our _____ Department, has received the highest honor that a teacher can receive. S/he has been selected by his/her peers and students in our senior class to be our Quality Staff Member of the Month. Those of you who are in Mr./Ms. _____'s class know that the honor is well deserved. Those of you who have yet to experience Mr./Ms. _____'s teaching are in for a treat." Awards have been made to the school's custodian, the head of security, guidance counselors, assistant principals, and numerous teachers. This recognition has increased staff morale.

At the request of our student leadership we have created various "Student Quality Bulletin Boards," recognizing student achievement in academics, sports, attendance, community service, work experience, acceptance to college, and the workplace.

MODIFICATION OF OTHER DEMING POINTS

In implementing Total Quality Education we have had to modify several other points:

POINT #13. "INSTITUTE A VIGOROUS PROGRAM OF EDUCATION AND RETRAINING."

Like most inner-city schools, we do not control our resources or time schedule. We are given a budget by the Board of Education. Our monies must be spent in the manner we have been directed to spend them. Monies for salaries must be used for salaries. Monies for security must be used for security. Money for computer software must be used for *software*. We cannot spend software money to buy computer *hardware*. We do not have sufficient resources to hire outside quality consultants. Whatever quality training that we have had has been provided by our quality coordinator or by quality consultants from National Westminster Bank USA or IBM, who have worked *pro bono*.

All of the Quality theorists agree that training is essential if total quality is to be implemented. In New York City that posed a major obstacle because schoolwide training is generally not done. Quality training is done during monthly faculty meetings. Only the teaching and guidance staff attend. Union rules permit meetings which last no longer than 45 minutes beyond a teacher's regular day. We squeeze training into our existing time frames. In the past, these meetings mainly dealt with administrative items. When schoolwide training meetings have been held, they have dealt with Board of Education mandated topics like HIV/AIDS, "No Guns in School," and racial harmony.

Funding for training is another limiting factor. There is extremely limited funding for teacher training in New York City high schools. Stated bluntly, school funding is not available in New York City high schools for staff training if it is not on the Board of Education's agenda.

Training of our students and parents has been even more difficult. At their request, we have given training sessions to our parents in our Parents Teacher Association meetings. These meetings are held once a month and there haven't been a constant core of attending parents.

The State of New York mandates material that must be taught in our courses. That material is tested in statewide examinations called Regents and Regents Competency Tests. Students who fail to pass these mandated examinations cannot receive a diploma. Total Quality isn't in the curricula. We have given Quality training assemblies to our students and have given Quality Academy Workshops to some of our students, but the training of most of our students has been limited.

POINT # 4. "END THE PRACTICE OF AWARDING BUSINESS ON PRICE TAG ALONE."

The New York City Board of Education determines, to a major degree, from whom we may purchase. The vast majority of our purchases are from Board of Education approved vendors. The policy stipulates buying from the lowest bidder, regardless of item quality or prior experience. We may not purchase either goods or services outside the approved vendor list.

POINT # 3. "CEASE DEPENDENCE ON MASS INSPECTION."

New York State has a test (Regents and Regents Competency Tests) and content-driven curriculum. High school students are required to take and pass 40 credits of class content and seven standardized examinations in order to receive a New York State diploma. We would be performing a disservice to our customers if we failed to have our students meet state mandated standards.

POINT # 10. "ELIMINATE SLOGANS, EXHORTATIONS, AND TARGETS FOR THE WORKFORCE."

Our students, according to some reports, watch seven hours of television a day. They are bombarded by commercials and slogans throughout their day. Slogans are a fact of student life in the 1990's.

If you were to come into Westinghouse, you would see a sign encouraging students to "Think 100%!" Many of our students merely attempt to pass classes. They think that merely passing ("Getting 65%") is good enough. Unfortunately, our floor (65%) becomes their ceiling. When they shoot too low, they fail. This creates rework. By using "Think 100%!" we are letting our students know that they should "be the best you can be." This is simply stating in another way that merely passing isn't good enough.

We have bulletin boards in our school recognizing student triumphs like 100% Attendance, Passing All Classes, Graduation, Acceptance to College or Full-time Employment, Receiving over an 85% average, being selected "Student of the Month," etc. We are aware slogans and bulletin boards, by themselves, will not provide a mechanism for change. They do provide a means of communicating with students of school-accepted values. Because of the nature of inner-city schools, some of our youngsters never achieve any success. We feel it is important to celebrate even the most minor of our student achievements.

CHALLENGES IN ADAPTING TQM TO EDUCATION

A number of companies and individuals have been generous in supplying Total Quality training to the principal, the Quality Coordinator, a number of our staff, some students, and a limited number of parents. We have been adapting corporate models to our educational mode. We have taken quality training in National Westminster Bank USA, Colgate-Palmolive, Motorola's Six Sigma, IBM Customer Driven Quality, and Digital Equipment programs.

Because public education is under special constraints, we have faced several major challenges in transferring Total

Quality Management concepts to education. Some of the unique challenges we face:

SCHOOLS DON'T CONTROL THEIR OWN RESOURCES

If industry faces a challenge, it is usually capable of diverting or increasing funding to deal with that challenge. Schools do not have that ability. Most of a school's funds are "earmarked" for specific needs. Money set aside for special education students cannot be used for regular education students. Monies designated for machinery or books cannot be used to hire a teacher no matter how great the need. Money that is saved must be spent or the school will not receive it in the following year. Unlike school districts, Westinghouse High School does not control its budget. We are assigned a budget by the Board of Education. Our flexibility regarding that budget is extremely limited.

EDUCATION IS NOT CONSIDERED VALUABLE OR VITAL BY SOME OF OUR INTERNAL CUSTOMERS

If somebody wants to have the service that a hotel supplies, the person can go to a hotel and choose which hotel based on the service supplied. There are a number of choices: The customer can choose, for example, among Marriott, Hilton, Sheraton, or Hyatt. The key is that the customer wants to have the service that a hotel supplies!

In contrast, schools have a number of customers who do not wish to have the service that a school supplies. Some students are in school for reasons other than receiving an education. Schools are warm, provide a social experience, and provide hot meals. Traditionally, student motivation has been achieved through extrinsic motivation (*i.e.*, teachers and parents pushing students to achieve). Because students are being pushed to do things that others want rather than what they want, they have become apathetic, do not study or do homework.

SCHOOLS HAVE LITTLE OR NO CONTROL OVER OUTSIDE CIRCUMSTANCES WHICH IMPACT ON EDUCATIONAL ENVIRONMENT

Students are not as sophisticated as most adults and bring their problems into a school (*e.g.,* AIDS or HIV, death, homelessness, divorce or separation of parents, poverty, alcohol and/or drug abuse, immigration). Many staff members haven't had to deal with similar problems in their own lives and therefore do not have the skills to deal with these complex student dilemmas.

Teachers do not control a student's life once they leave the school environment. Once a student leaves school, the pressures of peers, television, Nintendo, and sports compete for a student's time. For many youngsters, there isn't adult supervision at home to influence a child's decision of whether to watch television or do homework. Young children are frequently asked to face alone the problems of homelessness, family separation or divorce, poverty, alcohol or drug abuse.

THERE HAS BEEN A DECREASE IN SPENDING ON EDUCATION

Federal spending on education decreased during the Reagan and Bush administrations. While there has been increased spending in "real" dollars, this has generally been "earmarked" money; that is, money designated for specific purposes and goals. State and local expenditures have also decreased. New York State and New York City have cut $1.4 billion from the New York City educational budget in the past four years. Even though students with increased difficulties have increased during this period, schools have diminished resources to cope with the challenges.

THE GOALS OF THE SCHOOL ARE NOT DETERMINED WITHIN THE SCHOOL

Schools have become the cauldron of social and political experimentation. A school's goals are determined by politicians or business people without any input from those in the classrooms. Frequently, the goals are mixed, not stated or not clearly stated, and are frequently changing. Society has competing needs and has difficulty agreeing on educational priorities. New York City has 32 districts and 32 local school boards. The Central Board of Education controls the High School Division and helps to manage the 32 local boards. The local school boards and the central Board of Education are made up of people from diverse communities with diverse values and diverse demands.

The learning requirements of society are either not stated or are changing. In addition to providing instruction in reading, writing, and mathematics, schools are expected to deal with problems that other institutions within society are unwilling or unable to deal with. In the past, New York City schools have been asked to deal with social problems of homelessness, smoking, and the use of guns.

SOCIETY FREQUENTLY DOESN'T VALUE EDUCATION

In many communities across the United States, educational budgets must be approved by the voter. Few, if any, other individual government services require that vote. Voters approve highway spending, the cost of prisons, and governmental salaries under the umbrella of a "General Fund" vote. Since the voter must approve or disapprove the general budget as a whole, voter frustration is frequently demonstrated with the vote on education. Short-term concerns about having an adult body in a classroom creates difficulty hiring the best teachers coming into a field. Teachers' salaries are the largest cost item in education. Starting salaries in New York City of a teacher with a master's degree, is about $25,000. It is difficult to hire teachers who are computer literate when they can work in private industry at higher starting salaries.

TEACHERS AND SCHOOLS DIDN'T FEEL THE NEED TO CHANGE

A teacher's realm is the classroom. In that context, the teacher works in isolation. Whatever happens in that classroom is expected to be under the teacher's control. Teachers do not want the experience of running a school; that was not in the job description when they filed an application to teach.

Teachers are resistant to change. They don't have to change because they have job security under state tenure laws. Change hasn't done much for the classroom teacher. He or she has been told that the latest "flavor of the month" was going to solve all the educational challenges they face. They have seen each "solution" fail and are reticent to believe in another.

Inertia has become the operating system of the schools. Administrators and teachers often feel that, "I've got one foot out the door" or "I was here before this movement, I will be here after it passes."

SCHOOLS HAVE LONG OPERATED WITH A MONOPOLY MINDSET

The educational bureaucracy doesn't have a desire to change. Public schools have operated as monopolies since their inception. Schools are not operated for profit and do not feel that they have to change. Until recently, external demands for school improvement did not exist. Increased economic global pressure has caused that situation to change. In addition, school expenditures have increased without substantial increases in results. This has caused a spotlight to be thrown on the need to restructure.

TEACHER TRAINING HAS BEEN DONE OUTSIDE SCHOOLS

Many schools do not have either the budget or the experience to train their staffs. They have relied on outside consultants, buddy-teachers, or colleges and universities. A major challenge facing superintendents is what to do with student's when teachers are being trained in the latest techniques. Parents become resistant when schools are dismissed early so that teachers can be trained in school.

HUGE CUSTOMER TURNOVER RATE EVERY YEAR

The greatest difference between the industrial model and the educational model is the huge internal customer turnover in education. Our internal customers include our staff, our students and their parents.

It is not unusual for schools to have a 10% staff turnover every year. With this large a turnover, some schools have had difficulty hiring qualified teachers and have resorted to a variety of techniques to insure a teacher in every classroom. These techniques have included alternate requirements for classroom instructors and recertification of teachers in areas other than where they have been trained. For example, there is a great need for Special Education teachers. Physical Education teachers, who are in excess supply, have been assigned to Special Education classrooms with no or minimal training in Special Education. In New York City, 17,000 of the 60,000 teaching staff members are without proper state certification.

Teachers leave education for a variety of reasons:

- ◆ Low pay
- ◆ Dissatisfaction with the system
- ◆ Difficult working conditions
- ◆ Marriage or pregnancy
- ◆ Retirement and early buyouts

High schools face a student and parent turnover of at least 25% every year because of graduation. An extreme dropout problem exacerbates this situation. Imagine what impact there would be on Xerox if they experienced a 100% customer turnover rate every four years.

A FORGOTTEN MISSION

America's schools have forgotten their mission. They have become like many failing businesses, paying too little attention to their customers. America's schools have failed to focus on customer expectations, which is the essence of Total Quality Management and Total Quality Education. It is time to invert the pyramid (*see* illustration on next page) and redirect it as well.

Total Quality Education cannot be viewed as "a quick fix." Because it goes to the root cause of the challenge, it takes time for the process to work. It is not like an injection of a wonder drug. Once infused within the body, it takes time to start the healing. Those who look for an instant solution to the problems of education will be disappointed.

Total Quality Management does not provide a universal answer to the ills of education. Schools do not create all of the problems they are asked to solve. Problems of poverty, violence, drugs, and crime are not of the school's making. Total Quality Education permits a school to deal with problems within the school's scope of control.

Total Quality Education is not expensive. In the short run there may be additional costs incurred to provide training. In the long run there will be a more efficient delivery of services and a reduction in the costs of failure, classroom cutting, dropout rates, etc.

It is time to move to the third wave of quality. The Japanese rode the first wave when they adopted Total Quality Management as a way of living. American industry rode the second wave when it brought Total Quality Management back into this country in the 1980's. It is time for America's schools to start riding the crest of the third wave.

TRADITIONAL PYRAMID OF POWER

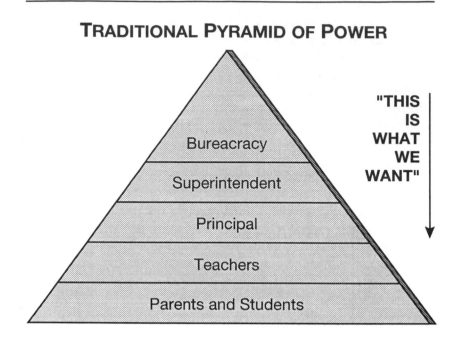

TOTAL QUALITY EDUCATION
TRANSFORMED PYRAMID OF POWER

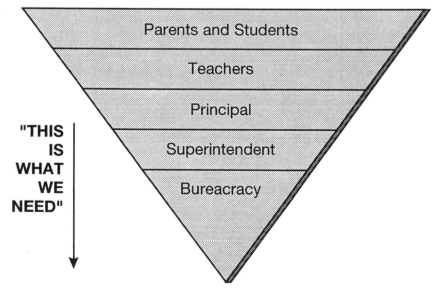

2

THE QUALITY TOOLS
AND TECHNIQUES*

A good deal of the innovation being done in the name of Quality in education is not measured. These innovations may be causing a positive change in performance and/or achievement or they may be doing harm. An important part of the Total Quality Management Process is a group of techniques and statistical tools which will serve as a "toolbox" and help provide the means that lead to quality improvement. The tools allow a visual presentation of the problems and their root causes, and therefore help the user propose solutions. Once presented with a challenge, the Total Quality practitioner need

---

* I am deeply indebted to my friend, Mark D. Gavoor for his assistance in writing this chapter. Mark provided suggestions and a clear method of presentation. He provided the "nuts and bolts" in the writing of this chapter. Mark has 15 years of experience in the quality movement working with Ford, General Dynamics, Rockwell, and TRW. He is currently Associate Director–Quality, Education, and Training in the Corporate Quality Office of the Colgate-Palmolive Company.

merely to reach into the "toolbox" and remove the appropriate tool to deal with the challenge. The "tools," by themselves, do not constitute Total Quality Management, but rather are a device to aid in the measurement of the process.

There are a large number of tools which industry has been using to gauge and measure the impact of the use of Total Quality techniques. Most early books talked about the "Seven Tools." Current books and theorists identify many more than seven. GOAL/QPC's *The Memory Jogger for Education* describes 10, while The Juran Institute's *Quality Improvement Pocket Guide* describes 19. David Langford, formerly of Mount Edgecombe High School, Sitka, Alaska, has compiled a list of 37 tools.

The bibliography (**Appendix C**) lists several superb books on the tools and their use. The purpose of this chapter is solely to introduce you to the tools which we have used. You are encouraged to refer to the books in the bibliography for a more extensive identification of the tools. The list is arranged in alphabetical order for ease of access.

ACTION PLAN

DESCRIPTION

An Action Plan is a listing of activities on a chart. (*See* next page for an example of an Action Plan chart format.) By identifying who is responsible, what resources are necessary and when actions are expected to be completed, a time-framed accountability is achieved. Formats may differ.

PROCEDURE

Step 1 Break the proposed actions into steps.

Step 2 Identify actions to be taken and the team or person responsible.

Step 3 Resources can mean additional people, additional telephones, or financial commitments which must be made.

Step 4 The list should be made as complete as possible.

```
┌─────────────────────────────┐
│         ACTION PLAN         │
└─────────────────────────────┘
```

ACTION PLAN REGARDING_____

Action to be Taken	Team/Person Responsible	Resources Needed	Target Dates Start/ End	Date Completed

SPECIFIC EDUCATIONAL APPLICATION AT GEORGE WESTINGHOUSE HIGH SCHOOL

The Quality Steering Committee was desirous of receiving additional applications of admission from our feeder schools. After brainstorming, we placed the items into an Action Plan.

ACTION PLAN

ACTION PLAN REGARDING Additional Student Applications

Action to be Taken	Team/Person Responsible	Resources Needed	Target Dates Start/End	Date Completed
Contact Parents Association (invitation to tour building)	PTA Team	Phone Bank Parent Members Coffee, Cookies	2/1	2/28
Call Principals of Feeder Schools (invitation to tour building)	Principal, Assistant Principals	Coffee, Cookies	2/1	2/28
Invite Counselors (invitation to tour building)	Guidance Dept.	Coffee, Cookies	3/30	6/30
Hold Trade Show (for feeder school students to see building and shops)	Trade Dept.	Personnel, Sec. Library, Postage, Drinks, Cookies	4/6, 7, 8	4/6, 7, 8

HINTS FOR ACTION PLANS

For a project like the one on the previous page, it is crucial that new teams, or their team leaders, conduct periodic checks on whether specific deadlines are likely to be met and, where necessary, provide additional resources in order to bring about the desired result.

BENCHMARKING

DESCRIPTION

Benchmarking has been used in industry to improve quality and lower costs. It is a technique which is a systematic process of comparing the best processes, strategies, and practices of successful organization's against one's own. Through the use of benchmarking, an organization is capable of improvement in its operation or delivery of service that could not otherwise be achieved. it is a technique for discovering what others have done and applying those techniques to one's own company. Organizations can "leap frog" steps that would normally be improved incrementally.

PROCEDURE

Step 1 Determine what operation or service you wish to benchmark.

Step 2 Determine who to benchmark. Investigate your own organization before selecting an outside or competitive benchmark.

Step 3 *Collect data* through the use of research, observation, surveys, interviews, professional literature, or contacts.

Step 4 *Analyze the data*. Establish criteria and a design a team to evaluate the data collected. Measure the gap between your organization and the organization being benchmarked.

Step 5 *Adapt the improvement* to fit your organization's culture and environment.

Step 6 *Implement the improvement and analyze the results.*

Step 7 If successful, "institutionalize" the innovation as an operating standard; if not, modify method and start cycle again.

SPECIFIC EDUCATIONAL APPLICATIONS

◆ Ask the school staff to identify the characteristics of an ideal school.

◆ Next to each item on the list have the staff identify a neighborhood school or business which they have heard or read about which fulfills that characteristic (*i.e.,* "Why is this school or business capable of higher achievement levels then we are?").

◆ Form teams to develop action plans to "benchmark" that characteristic from the individual business or school. There are many areas which a school might wish to benchmark including:

- admissions
- alumni
- athletics
- budgeting
- career and college planning
- collection and distribution of mail
- counseling
- discharging of students
- food service
- hiring of personnel
- inventory control
- operation of telephone systems
- parking
- purchasing
- repairs of school property
- report cards
- school store operations
- security

- student activities
- use of facilities

HINTS FOR BENCHMARKING

◆ Do not confine your benchmarking to educational institutions. Xerox benchmarked L.L. Bean in the area of warehousing. Federal Express has made impressive inroads in dealing with customer satisfaction.

◆ Do not forget to look in your own organization first. One department may be able to benchmark another. One team of secretaries may be able to learn from another team of secretaries.

◆ Ask:
  - Who is the best in the field?
  - What techniques do they use to achieve this result?
  - How can we adapt what they do to our school/district?

◆ One school's techniques will have to be adapted to another's culture. A template of merely copying another company will not produce the desired results.

BRAINSTORMING

DESCRIPTION

Brainstorming is a well-known technique for teams to generate and clarify a list of ideas. Brainstorming relies heavily on one idea generating other ideas so that the team has a wealth of information with which to move forward. Brainstorming can be used to generate improvement ideas, potential causes for, or solutions to, problems involving customer wants and needs. The process should be used as a form of free association to generate as many ideas as possible.

PROCEDURE

Step 1 Discuss and clarify the purpose of brainstorming
The facilitator should write the purpose on a chalkboard or newsprint.

Step 2 Generate ideas
There are three methods for idea generation. Each method requires private individual brainstorming, listing preliminary ideas on paper or card. The three methods are:

a. *Structured Brainstorming:* The facilitator goes around the table asking each team member to contribute an idea from their list. As the group hears other members' suggestions, it should stimulate them to think of additional proposals. The process continues until there are no additional ideas. If team members do not have an idea, they may pass, but can contribute later when their turn comes again. This continues until there aren't any other ideas.

b. *"The Popcorn Method:"* This technique has the facilitator open the brainstorming to anyone who "pops up" with an idea.

c. *"Idea Grouping"* or *"Affinity Grouping:"* The ideas are developed individually in a 20–30 minute session. The ideas are then written on "Post-its" (one idea per "Post-it"). Team members put their "Post-its" out on a table or flip chart, where the team organizes them into groupings which appear to belong together or have an affinity for each other. (Hence the name of "Affinity Diagram" for the product of the effort.) Each grouping is then given a title by which the individual ideas can be identified. If the team feels that an idea belongs under more than one title or "header," duplicate "Post-its" should be made.

◆ **Display**
All ideas and thoughts should be centrally displayed.

◆ **Evaluate and Prioritize**
When there aren't any more ideas, the facilitator leads the team discussion, evaluating and prioritizing the ideas utilizing any one of a variety of Total Quality tools and techniques.

HINTS ON BRAINSTORMING

◆ Ideas should not be criticized or discussed until all of the ideas are generated. This is important because oftentimes the most inane, humorous, or off-the-wall comment generates additional ideas in others.

◆ It is suggested that method 2a be used with teams new to the process and, perhaps, to each other. This will encourage the entire team participates rather than Brainstorming being dominated by a few, more vocal team members.

CAUSE AND EFFECT DIAGRAM

DESCRIPTION

The Cause and Effect Diagram is a brainstorming tool used in process improvement and problem solving. Teams use the Cause and Effect Diagram to brainstorm and provide an initial sort on the possible cause of a particular concern, problemor effect. Once the possible causes are brainstormed, the team can discuss them, prioritize them by importance, and determine further actions with the goal of determining the root causes of the effect.

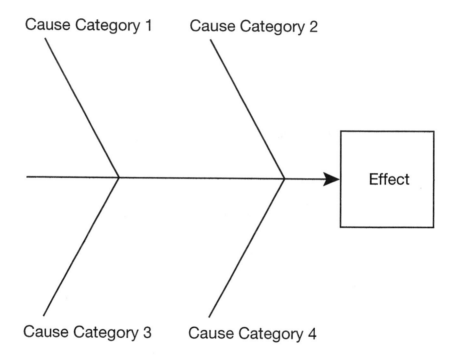

The Cause and Effect Diagram is also known as the Fishbone Diagram, due to its shape, and the Ishikawa Diagram, due to Kaoru Ishikawa, the Japanese quality expert who formalized the tool in 1953.

PROCEDURE

Step 1 Discuss the effect, concern or problem, and agree on the wording of the concern.

Step 2 Sketch out the main bones of the fishbone, writing the effect in the box at the right.

Step 3 Determine the main Cause Categories or "headers.". The team can utilize the classic "4 M's" or "4 P's" or make up their own. The main Cause Categories should be the best that apply to the effect in question.

4 M's	*4P's*
Method	Policies
Manpower	Procedures
Material	People
Machines (Equipment)	Plant (Facilities)

Step 4 Brainstorm the possible causes. Use the Cause Categories to guide the brainstorming process. Obey the general rules of brainstorming (*i.e.,* Record all ideas as they are raised. No ideas should be judged at this point.). The ideas should be written as branches to the main bone. Ideas subordinate to other ideas are record on sub-branches to the main idea.

SPECIFIC EDUCATIONAL APPLICATIONS

◆ The Quality Steering Committee wanted to identify the root causes for student failure at Westinghouse. The first diagram (Lack of Quality in Schools), found on page 33, is one example of our use of the Cause and Effect Diagram.

◆ The second Cause and Effect Diagram (Variation in Exam Grades), found on page 34, was developed to help explain the variation in examination grades. It was developed by students in Jeanne Benecke's math classrooms.

◆ The third Cause and Effect Diagram (Lack of Quality in Schools), found on page 35, was developed by the students in the Total Quality Classroom. After brainstorming about why America has had limited quality in schools, they used their "fishbone diagram" to visually present the ideas that they brainstormed.

HINTS FOR CAUSE AND EFFECT DIAGRAMS

◆ A separate Cause and Effect Diagram should be developed for each separate effect.

◆ As the team progresses, the Cause and Effect Diagram should be updated to reflect new learnings.

◆ Team members should all have a copy of the Cause and Effect Diagram.

CHECKLIST

DESCRIPTION

A checklist is a very simple and useful tool. It is simply a list of things that must be done. Complex tasks are made up of many easy activities. By listing all of these activities on a checklist, a team or person charged with the task can ensure that each activity gets accomplished. By breaking down the activities, an apparently overwhelming task is broken down to its simpler components.

CAUSE AND EFFECT DIAGRAM: LACK OF QUALITY IN SCHOOLS

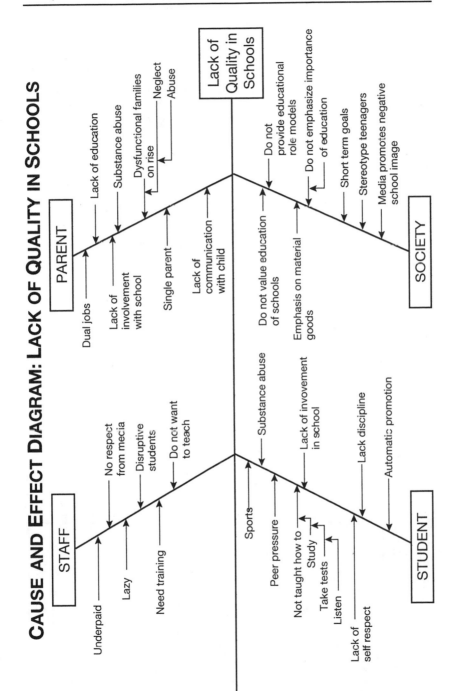

CAUSE AND EFFECT DIAGRAM: VARIATION IN EXAM GRADES

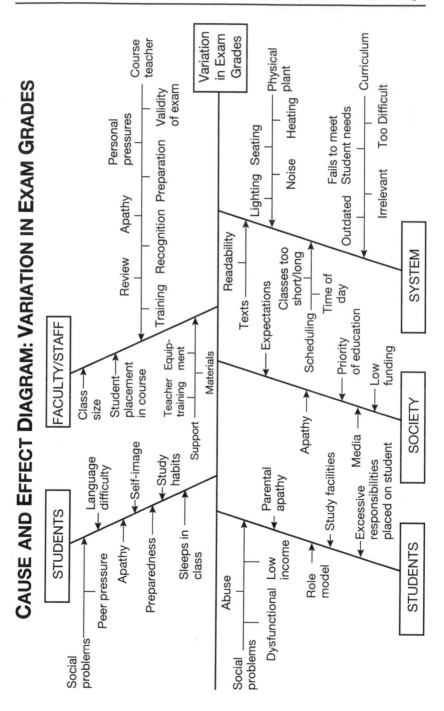

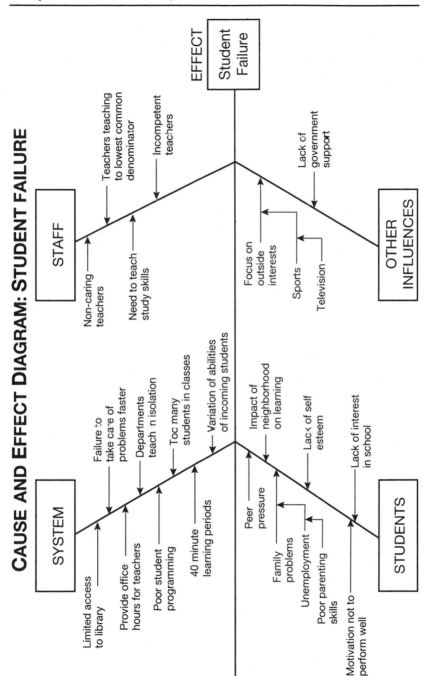

CAUSE AND EFFECT DIAGRAM: STUDENT FAILURE

EFFECT — Student Failure

STAFF
- Non-caring teachers
- Teachers teaching to lowest common denominator
- Need to teach study skills
- Incompetent teachers

SYSTEM
- Limited access to library
- Provide office hours for teachers
- Failure to take care of problems faster
- Departments teach in isolation
- Poor student programming
- Too many students in classes
- 40 minute learning periods
- Variation of abilities of incoming students

OTHER INFLUENCES
- Focus on outside interests
- Sports
- Television
- Lack of government support

STUDENTS
- Peer pressure
- Impact of neighborhood on learning
- Family problems
- Unemployment
- Lack of self esteem
- Poor parenting skills
- Motivation not to perform well
- Lack of interest in school

The philosophy behind a checklist is equally simple. Take time, in a period of calm, to list, prioritize, sequence, and assign responsibilities to all the activities (sub-tasks) of a complex task. In this way, the checklist can guide an individual or team, save time, and help prevent any activity from being inadvertently ignored or forgotten. Most of us use a packing checklist before leaving for vacation. Aircraft crews use checklists to coordinate the complex activities necessary for safe and successful flights.

PROCEDURE

Step 1 Discuss and clearly define the task for which the checklist is being created.

Step 2 Brainstorm all of the activities (sub-tasks) associated with the task.

Step 3 These activities must be:
- sequenced
- prioritized
- assigned to individuals/teams to complete.

Step 4 The final list should be printed, used in a dry run and revised as necessary.

SPECIFIC EDUCATIONAL APPLICATION AT GEORGE WESTINGHOUSE HIGH SCHOOL

Opening Day Procedure

☐ Students admitted
☐ Signs directing students
☐ Report cards distributed
☐ Security assigned
☐ Program cards distributed
☐ Transportation passes distributed
☐ Lunch passes distributed
☐ Inform students of schedule for the rest of the week
☐ Distribution of school calendar for school year
☐ Process for dealing with late arriving students
☐ Process for dealing with absent students
☐ Greetings from Principal
☐ Process for dismissal of students
☐ Assign Counselors to be available for change of programs
☐ Assign personnel to process new admittees to school

FLOW CHART

DESCRIPTION

Total Quality focuses on unifying the people of an organization into teams that work to improve the various processes of that organization. Flow charts are an excellent way to depict graphically the sequences of activities which make up the process. By using a visual representation of the steps in a process, an understanding is achieved of how the process actually works. By examining how the process steps relate to each other, potential sources of problems can be seen and eliminated.

When developing a flow chart of a process in a team setting, it should become clear that:

- ◆ There are many different views of how the process works.
- ◆ The process is more complex than any of the team members had expected.

It is critical that a team charged with improving a process understand the process in the same way. Developing a flow chart together brings the team this collective understanding.

PROCEDURE

Step 1 The process start and stop points must be clearly defined. The following questions must be clarified:
- What events designate the start of the process?
- What event, products, or services signify the completion of the process?

Step 2 Brainstorming the set of events or activities which make up the process. Include the key decision points and "what ifs." A "what if" in this case is the answer to the following types of questions:
- *What if* the person responsible for handling an activity is at lunch, on vacation, out ill, or otherwise not available?
- *What if* the information necessary to complete an activity is not available?

Step 3 Review and refine the activities brainstormed and then record them on index cards or "Post-its" using the following symbols.

Start/Stop

Process Step or Activity

Decision

Step 4 Arrange the process steps on a table or central display in the order in which the activities actually occur. Connect the activities with arrows (—→) to show the flow of the activities.

Step 5 Clean-up, redraw, and distribute the final flow chart.

FLOW CHART: INSTRUCTIONAL PROCESS AT GEORGE WESTINGHOUSE HIGH SCHOOL

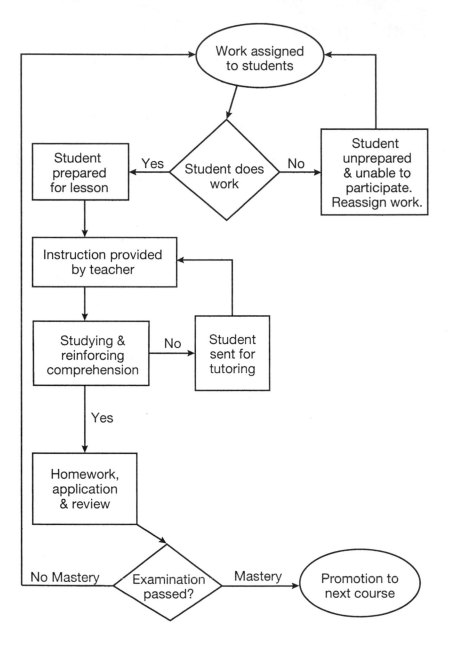

HINTS ON FLOW CHARTING

- ◆ It is best to have only one arrow coming into an activity.

- ◆ For an activity that has multiple in or out arrows, try breaking down the activity into multiple activities and decisions.

- ◆ Most people when asked to explain how a process works explain something simple and linear. Usually all the contingency decisions (the "what ifs") are left out. When a team flows out the process in detail, it is often astounding to the team how nonlinear the process is.

- ◆ The team should highlight an ideal process flow and begin to study all other activities to develop countermeasures and process changes which keep the process from performing optimally.

- ◆ Given a chain of activities, unnecessary activities should be eliminated or tasks should be done in parallel to save time.

PARETO CHARTS

DESCRIPTION

The primary use of Pareto Analysis is to help a team collect problem, symptom, or defect data from a process, assign that data to individual root causes, and then rank-order those root causes. The data is displayed as a bar graph with the information displayed in descending order of defect incidence. Once a team knows the problem sources of greatest significance in a process, it can address them first, leaving the less significant items for later. In this way, the team can focus on items which will provide the greatest pay back. Pareto Analysis is central to any problem-solving or process improvement activity.

Pareto Charts are named for the Italian economist Wilfredo Pareto. In 1897, Pareto showed that the distribution of wealth was uneven: 80% of the wealth was in the hands of 20% of the population.

Dr. Joseph J. Juran noted that this 80/20 rule also generally applies to management problems and, especially, process improvement situations. Dr. Juran's Pareto Rule states that "80% of the trouble in a process or system stems from 20% of the problems." He urges practitioners to concentrate on the "vital few" problems and not be distracted by those of lesser importance ("the useful many"). Simply stated, 20% of the problem causes account for 80% of the problem symptoms in a process. By concentrating on the 20% it is possible to get maximum improvement with the least effort!

PROCEDURE

Step 1 Determine the characteristic (defects, cost, subjects, failure, "classroom cutting") to be studied.

Step 2 Brainstorm the classifications of the main characteristic to be evaluated (*e.g.*, Student Academic Failures by Subject: English, Foreign Language, Math, Physical Education, Science, and Social Studies).

Step 3 Determine the time period and method of data collection.

Step 4 Collect the data.

Step 5 Create a Pareto Diagram
   a. Plot as a bar chart of the number of failures (vertical axis) against the individual academic subjects (horizontal axis). The scale for the number of failures should be from 0 to the total number of failures reported.
   b. Create another vertical axis, on the right side, for cumulative percentage. Draw a line graph for cumulative percentage with the observation for each classification being above the

right hand edge to the bar for that classification. Check to see if the data conforms with the Pareto Rule.

SPECIFIC EDUCATIONAL APPLICATIONS AT GEORGE WESTINGHOUSE HIGH SCHOOL

Our counselors informed us that, at the beginning of the term, they were overwhelmed with work. They felt that the most time-consuming factor was the program changes that had to be made. As a result of brainstorming, we discovered that some of our students went to summer school and therefore had to be reprogrammed. We also had new admissions who had to be seen. Many parents came into school and wanted to talk to the counselors.

We decided to analyze the program change requests for the time period September 20, 1993, to October 30, 1993:

Program Requests Processed 9/20/93–10/30/93

Total Number Processed = 361 (out of a student population of 1761)
Percentage Processed = 21.2%
Number Processed more than once = 12 (3.2%)
Number of requests to drop last period = 85 (22.8%)

Requests by type		
Switch period or teacher only		102 (27.3%)
Requested by Assistant Principals		64 (17.7%)
Math	48	
Shop	11	
English	3	
Social Studies	2	
Going into Co-op Program		38 (10.5%)
Drop lunch period		31 (8.6%)
Wrong Class Programmed		30 (8.3%)
(Same department, different course)		
To give "high risk" students a program		
after counseling		30 (8.3%)
Passed in summer school		23 (6.4%)
From holding power to full program		22 (6.1%)
Change shop		21 (5.8%)
TOTAL		**361**

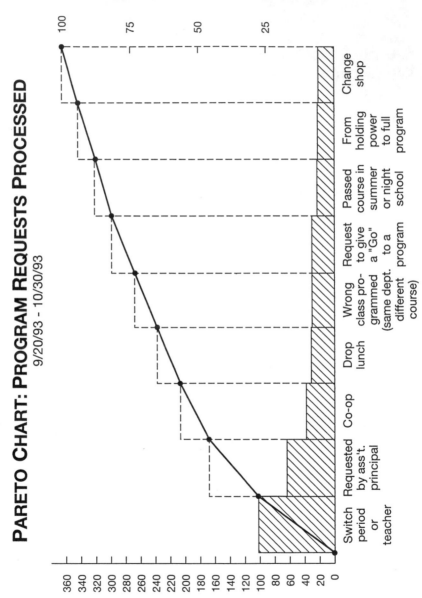

We were also interested in visually showing Assistant Principals of Supervision what academic courses our senior students failed to master. We selected the 6-week marking period of May 17, 1993–June 25, 1993:

Mathematics	180 student failures	(45.0%)
Science	96 student failures	(24.0%)
Social Studies	42 student failures	(10.5%)
English	36 student failures	(9.0%)
Foreign Language	28 student failures	(7.0%)
Physical Education	18 student failures	(4.5%)
TOTAL	**400**	

Based on the information obtained, the Mathematics and Science Departments went on to analyze the reasons that senior students disproportionally failed their courses. They interviewed the seniors, distributed surveys, and based on the information gathered, determined that additional tutorial help should be offered to the seniors. The Pareto Chart analysis of the courses failed by students appears on the next page.

HINTS ON PARETO CHARTS

 ◆ On the Pareto Diagram, the bar graphs should be touching.

 ◆ In *Statistical Methods for Quality Improvement*, edited by Hitushi Kume, there are two types of Pareto Diagrams:
   • *by Phenomena* which help refine and stratify the nature of quality concerns, providing opportunities for much more detail to be incorporated into the chart.
   • *by Cause* which help determine the root causes.

PARETO CHART: COURSES FAILED BY STUDENTS

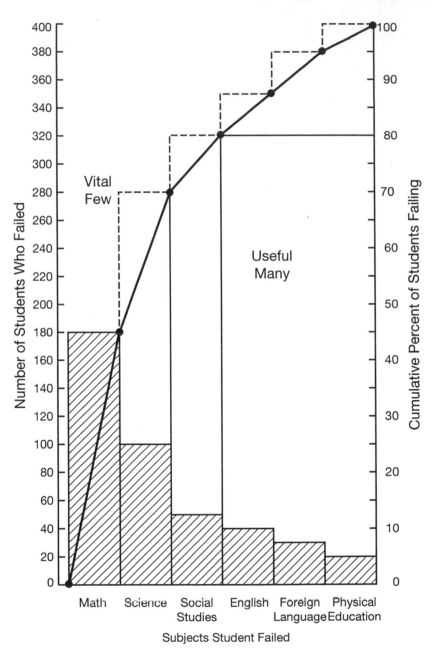

PLAN-DO-CHECK-ACT (PDCA) OR PLAN-DO-STUDY-ACT (PDSA) CYCLE OR SHEWART/DEMING CYCLE

DESCRIPTION

The Total Quality Management process emphasizes a cyclical process for the continuous improvement of a system, rather than an approach with a beginning, middle, and end. Originally conceived in 1939 by Walter A. Shewart, Dr. Deming's friend and mentor, the four-step Plan-Do-Check-Act (PDCA) cycle was later changed by Dr. Deming to Plan-Do-Study-Act (PDSA). Either version is recognized by TQM practitioners who refer to the process as either the PDCA, PDSA, Shewaart, Deming, or Shewart/Deming Cycle.

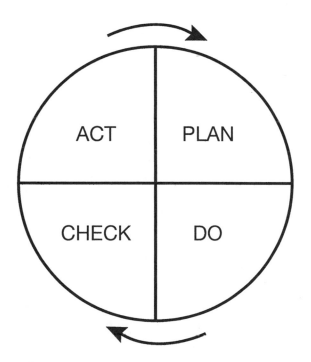

PROCEDURE

Step 1 **PLAN**: The team should develop a plan to improve a process. The plan should seek input from customers, suppliers, workers and top management.

Step 2 **DO**: Carry out the change, preferably on a small scale.

Step 3 **CHECK**: Check the results from the changes implemented. Did the changes work well? What must be improved in order to do a better job?

Step 4 **ACT**: Adopt or abandon the change as a part of the process. Repeat the cycle to see the impact of the change and to make the process more successful.

SCATTER DIAGRAM

DESCRIPTION

A Scatter diagram allows the user to determine the existence, and if present, assess the strength of the relationship between two variables. The diagram is a plot of data points in which different values of one variable are compared with the corresponding values of another variable. The shape of the scattering of data points indicates if the two variables are related and, if so, to what degree. If they are related, the points will be clustered closely and will define a line. Depending upon the direction of the line, either a positive or negative correlation exists.

PROCEDURE

Step 1 Use the horizontal axis to display the values of one variable and the vertical axis to display the values of the other variable.

Step 2 Record the values of each variable on the appropriate axis. Plot a large enough number of data points so as to be able to determine if a relationship exists. The data points will fall randomly in the absence of any relationship.

Step 3 Notice the strength of the relationship between the two variables (as the angle the resultant line makes with the horizontal or vertical axis of the diagram).

Step 4 In a positive correlation, the values of either variable will increase as the other increases, and will decrease as the other decreases. Stated in another way, those points in the lower left hand corner need improvement. Those in the upper right hand corner are excellent.

SPECIFIC EDUCATION APPLICATION AT GEORGE WESTINGHOUSE HIGH SCHOOL*

We were interested in seeing if there was a correlation between completed homework assignments and test grades. Jeanne Benecke ran a series of scatter diagrams. On the next page is a scatter diagram which shows a high positive correlation between completed homeworks and grades on a test.

---

* I am deeply indebted to Jeanne Benecke, Westinghouse's Statistical Quality Coordinator, for the suggestions, recommendations, and charts she supplied for this chapter.

SCATTER DIAGRAM: EXAM GRADES AND NUMBER OF HOMEWORKS COMPLETED
(Data from Exam 4/20/93)

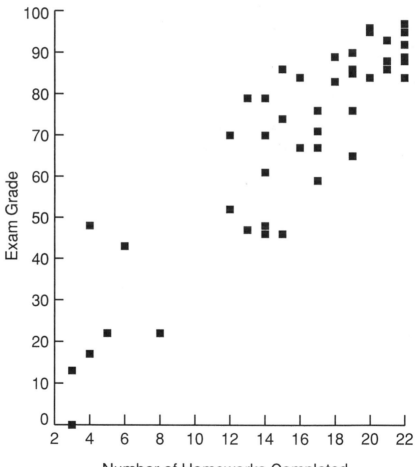

3

GETTING TO KNOW GEORGE WESTINGHOUSE VOC/TECH HIGH SCHOOL

When we began implementing Total Quality at Westinghouse we came to realize that we faced challenges unique to our city and our school. While other schools face similar challenges, the combination is unique with us.

OUR STUDENTS

Westinghouse draws students from 70 different "feeder" junior high schools and intermediate schools. Although the school is open to all city residents, most of our students reside in the inner-city neighborhoods of Brooklyn. Some of our students travel from the outer boroughs of Staten Island and the Bronx. For those students, the trip to Westinghouse can take up to 2 hours each way on either public subways or buses.

We had 302 entering students in September, 1993. The largest feeder school sent 23 students to our entering ninth and tenth grades. The next six largest feeder schools sent between 11 and 19 students. Sixty-three schools sent less than 10 students. These students came to Westinghouse with varying degrees of reading and mathematics abilities. One hundred sixty-seven entered with scores below reading average as demonstrated on the Degrees of Reading Power Examination. Almost 4% (3.977%) had not taken any reading test in their intermediate or junior high school. Almost 10% (9.27%) of our 1993 entering class demonstrated "Limited English Proficiency." Many of our students come from homes where a language other than English is spoken. Some of them come from homes where English is not spoken at all. In order to educate them, we need to bring them all to the same starting position.

Of the approximately 1,700 students currently enrolled (1993):

- ◆ 76% are black;
- ◆ 20% are Latino;
- ◆ almost 2½% are Asian;
- ◆ 32 students are white;
- ◆ 25% are female.
- ◆ Many of our students come from single-parent low income families.
- ◆ Over 50% are eligible for the free lunch program (1992).
- ◆ Almost one-half of Westinghouse's graduates will be the first in their families to obtain a high school diploma.

◆ Most students are coming from single-parent families.

Students are sent to our school for a variety of reasons. Some parents wish their children to learn a trade or skill. Many do not want their children in neighborhood schools because of their fear of crime, violence, or a poor educational environment. Others wish to remove their children from the peers with whom they grew up. Still others wish to remove their children from the neighborhoods where they live. All of these factors must be weighed against their children riding on the New York City subway system for an average of 45 minutes each way to school.

Westinghouse has problems typical of many inner-city schools. Many students enter our school with a lack of motivation, a history of educational failure, and a low self-esteem.

A recent Federal study stated that about 14½% of the country lived in poverty. Westinghouse's student population has a concentration of 62% living in poverty.

Our students live with violence. We estimate that we have attended over 50 funerals in the past 7 years for students who have died in their neighborhoods. Recently, one of our students died on their way to get a haircut.

Students who attend our school must earn an academic as well as a vocational diploma. They must pass 4 years of English, 4 years of Social Studies, 2 years of mathematics and science, 1 year of foreign language, a term of hygiene and music, and 4 years of physical education. Their school day is generally longer than that of a student who attends a comprehensive school. Students in vocational high school must take and pass all of the New York State required examinations that academic students must pass.

Beginning on the next page is a chart showing our school's performance in various areas during four school years. You will see progress in many, but not all, categories.

OVERVIEW & SUMMARY OF PERFORMANCE INDICATORS
George Westinghouse
Vocational & Technical High School
(Information supplied by the Board of Education
& Westinghouse High School)

Years:	1989–90	1990–91	1991–92	1992–93
REGISTERS				
General Ed.	1664	1593	1641	1758
Special Ed.	160	150	143	136
TOTAL	**1824**	**1743**	**1784**	**1894**
SOCIO-ECONOMIC				
Free-Reduced Lunch	31.9%	37.4%	37.1%	30.7%
Low Income	31.9%	37.4%	62.4%	61.6%
ANNUAL ATTENDANCE				
General Ed.	86.1%	84.1%	86.9%	84.1%
Special Ed.	72.8%	72.7%	78.3%	76.7%
TOTAL	**85.0%**	**83.2%**	**86.3%**	**83.6%**
ETHNICITY				
Alaskan & Am. Indian	0.3%	0.1%	0.0%	0.1%
Asian	1.9%	2.2%	2.6%	2.4%
Hispanic	21.9%	21.2%	21.0%	20.0%
Black	75.4%	76.0%	75.2%	75.9%
White	0.5%	0.5%	1.2%	1.7%

Years:	1989–90	1990–91	1991–92	1992–93
INCIDENTS REPORTED BY PRINCIPAL[1]				
	79	29	56	93
REGENTS EXAMINATION (PASSING)[2]				
English	64.1%	57.4%	37.4%	62.8%
U.S. History	64.3%	42.6%	51.4%	62.5%
Global Studies	46.7%	37.2%	71.4%	62.5%
Seq. Math I	36.0%	39.7%	50.4%	35.6%
Seq. Math II	46.6%	41.6%	42.3%	35.6%
Seq. Math III	56.4%	26.8%	57.6%	51.4%
Biology	40.0%	70.4%	50.0%	40.0%
Chemistry	90.0%	[3]	50.0%	46.2%
Physics	79.2%	87.5%	70.4%	71.4%
Earth Science	[3]	[3]	[3]	71.4%
REGENTS COMPETENCY EXAMINATIONS (PASSING)				
Reading	87.8%	89.3%	83.2%	93.0%[4]
Mathematics	34.9%	45.3%	49.5%	46.5%[4]
Writing	68.9%	78.2%	65.7%	[3]
Science	50.2%	51.9%	47.1%	34.9%[4]
U.S. History	74.8%	70.7%	64.5%	66.7%[4]
Global Studies	50.8%	31.7%	36.4%	17.3%[4]

Years:	1989–90	1990–91	1991–92	1992–93

OCCUPATIONAL EDUCATION PROFICIENCY EXAMINATION (PASSING)

	67.8%	61.1%	70.0%	[3]

DEGREES OF READING POWER EXAMINATION (DRP) (PERCENTAGE ABOVE 50% ILE)

Grade 9	44.9%	59.5%	40.4%	50.4%
Grade 10	55.7%	60.1%	57.5%	68.3%

SCHOLASTIC APTITUDE TEST

# Taking	71	98	91	[3]
Verbal Mean	328	319	318	[3]
Math Mean	391	393	354	[3]

GRADUATES GOING ON TO HIGHER LEARNING

	68.9%	69%	72.1%	

STUDENT DROPOUT RATE

	—	7.8%	5.3%	2.1%

Notes

[1] Incidents are reported to the superintendent for fighting, weapon possession, drug possession,etc.

[2] Regents examinatons are the highest level of New York State standardized examinations. Students must pass either seven Regents Examinations or seven Regents Competency Examinations in order to receive a New York State Diploma.

[3] Either no exam was given or results were not reported back to the school.

[4] Partial figures for the year.

OUR PARENTS

Most of our parents are single—slightly over 50% graduated from high school. They run their own household, work, and raise other children in addition to the one they have in Westinghouse. They come home from work exhausted and must prepare dinner. For some of them, their child's attendance or achievement in high school is at the end of a long list of other obligations.

OUR BUDGET

Budget cuts in the past 4 years have ranged from 3% to 12¾% (1993). These cuts have resulted in having 13 fewer staff members with approximately the same number of students. Additionally, it means that we have fewer supplies and less equipment. Inflation has also decreased our ability to purchase supplies and equipment.

SUPPORT FROM THE BUREAUCRACY

Most schools which have embarked on the Total Quality journey have done so with the active support and cooperation of the superintendent and the Board of Education. The central Board of Education and our Superintendent have not supplied us with additional personnel or resources to aid Westinghouse in its quality journey.

OUR STAFF

Many of the teachers in our school have been in "the House" for most of their teaching careers and most will retire from Westinghouse. Few teachers transfer to other schools and we have 13 Westinghouse alumni who have returned to teach in the "House."

Our senior staff members, most with over 20 years of experience, are skeptical of educational innovation, having gone through various educational proposals which have had little, no, or negative impact in the classroom. In order to reduce the cost of running the schools, in 1990 the Board of Education offered an "early buyout." Eight percent of our staff took the buyout. Their replacements, while more responsive to change, have less training in most school matters. The United Federation of Teachers is the second largest teacher union local in the country. Its contract imposes rules regarding the number and length of training meetings. We are limited to a maximum of two 45-minute meetings a month. One meeting is for the entire faculty and other is for instructional departments. These meetings are held on Mondays.

OUR SCHOOL

George Westinghouse Vocational and Technical High School is located in the heart of downtown Brooklyn. Downtown Brooklyn is undergoing an industrial renaissance. A new industrial complex, Metrotech, is being built. Presently housed in the complex are New York Telephone Company, Brooklyn Union Gas Company, Consolidated Edison, and the Chase Manhattan Bank.

We share a common auditorium with New York City Technical College and are across the street from Polytechnic University (formerly Brooklyn Polytechnic).

Westinghouse is neither a magnet school nor does it administer a test for entry. Any student who desires can attend by filing an application with the Board of Education. The school then selects from the applications based on capacity for a specific technical or vocational program.

Westinghouse High School has been in existence for 74 years. It is presently housed in two connected structures. The "old building," a former elementary school, houses the academic classrooms and a few industrial laboratories. The "new building" contains the remaining laboratories.

Like most schools in the inner-city, the school is in need of repairs and painting. There are holes in some ceilings and the floor tiles are coming up in some of the classrooms. In spite of the needed repairs, Westinghouse is well maintained and we take pride in our well-kept school. Some of the public address speakers in classrooms do not work. We have waited more than 12 years for their repair. The school has newly installed security devices, including electronic door locks and metal detectors.

As a vocational school, Westinghouse has advantages over neighborhood comprehensive schools. Once a student gets a diploma from an academic school, he or she must acquire the skills that a vocational student already possesses. A vocational school diploma provides the academic preparation and the skills to enter the workforce. Most of our students (or their parents) want to come to our school. Some students come to avoid going to a neighborhood school and not because they wish to obtain vocational training. If a student does not do the work we require, we can request that he or she return to his "zoned" high school.

As a vocational high school, Westinghouse has made some connections to the business community and many of the staff were receptive to trying business practices which have worked.

When the principal and I arrived at Westinghouse in 1987, the school had a neutral reputation. We were neither the best school in the city nor its worst. Principal Lewis A. Rappaport liked to say we were "the best kept secret in Brooklyn."

One of our first tasks upon arriving at Westinghouse was to build a good reputation among the incoming business community, a demoralized staff, incoming students and their parents. During the summer of 1988, we wrote a promotional piece based on a model developed by our Special Events Coordinator. The promotional piece helped make Westinghouse known to the businesspeople. It also let our "feeder schools" know who we were and what we had to offer. We entered the piece in the New York State "Occolades" Award where it won an Honorable Mention in the promotional piece category.

Over 150 staff members, many of who come from some of private industry's most prestigious firms, guide students in 11 different trade and technical programs, ranging from optical mechanics to computer programming. According to a list compiled by the Bureau of Labor Statistics in 1986, Westinghouse is preparing students for 8 of the top 20 fastest growing career areas.

Westinghouse's programs frequently incorporate classroom study with field experience. We have one of the largest co-op programs in the New York City metropolitan area. Our co-op students alternate 1 week of school with 1 week of work. In 1984, President Ronald Reagan honored the school with a presidential citation for our "Partners for the Advancement of Electronics Program."

The school supports several athletic teams, including baseball, track, softball, handball, and soccer. A number of students are active in numerous extracurricular activities such as our nationally recognized "Senior Citizen Escort Service" and Darts, Chess, Computers, Leadership, Math, Optical, Asian and African-American Culture.

We were fortunate in finding Robert (Bob) Cox, an executive on loan from National Westminster Bank USA, who was working at the Brooklyn Chamber of Commerce. Bob found an advertising company which was willing to do the lay out for the promotional piece found in Appendix A. Bob arranged for Brooklyn Union Gas to pay their fee. We found a printer who supplied us with 5,000 pro bono copies.

Bob Cox also introduced us to the people at National Westminister Bank USA. "Nat West" prides itself on being a "Quality bank." If a teller doesn't greet you when you come in, the bank will give you money. If they don't notify you about a loan request in a certain period of time, you receive $10. The concept of quality interested the principal and I. We went to the New York City headquarters of the bank and took quality training. We were so impressed that we asked if we could bring some of our staff and use them to "turnkey" other staff members. The people at the bank graciously agreed. Twenty-seven staff members went for the training. National Westminster Bank also agreed to train student members of our Leadership Class.

At the beginning of the new school year, Steve Michaels of the bank agreed to give a workshop to our entire staff. As a result of the training, staff interest was raised and we began our "Quality Staff Member of the Month" program using the bank's model.

Our interest was piqued. Using Mr. Michaels' suggestions, we started reading books about quality (*e.g., Quality is Free* by Phillip R. Crosby). We attended the American Society of Quality Award Meeting held to announce National Quality Month (1988) .

In November 1990, the author attended a GOAL/QPC meeting in Boston. Larrae Rocheleau, the Superintendent of

Mount Edgecombe High School, Sitka, Alaska, was one of the presenters. I sat in on Larrae's workshop and spoke to him afterward. I also went with him to a NEQI (National Education Quality Initiative) meeting and met other educators who were getting involved in the process.

Afterward, I met with Principal Rappaport. He agreed that we should either get totally involved with the process or get out. Buying a small piece, as we had done with recognition and reward, would not work.

From November 1990 until January 30, 1991, we read as many quality books as we could. On January 30, 1991, we introduced Total Quality Management to the faculty of Westinghouse.

We wanted to know what the staff felt about a number of items. On January 30, 1991, we distributed this survey:

Please do not put your name on this form and answer as honestly as possible.

1. How would you define Westinghouse as a school (compared to other high schools in New York City)? (Circle one.)
    Superior
    Above average
    Average
    Below average
    Far below average

2. What factors do you feel hold Westinghouse back from being a quality school? (Circle all that apply.)
    The educational system
    The principal
    The administration (assistant principals and department
        coordinators)
    The teachers
    The students
    The parents
    The outside community (*e.g.*, the media)
    Other _____

3. Regarding students (check only one):
    They are not capable of learning.
    They are capable of learning.
    They are capable of learning but don't try.

4. Regarding parents (check only one):
   Most couldn't care less.
   Most are cooperative if contacted and give teachers' support.

5. Regarding teachers (check only one):
   Most couldn't care less.
   Most are concerned but lack the techniques to handle problems.

6. Regarding the principal and the administration (check only one):
   They don't care.
   They're trying but lack techniques.

7. The greatest impediment to success at Westinghouse is (check only one):
   The educational system
   The principal
   The administration (assistant principals and department coordinators)
   The teachers
   The students
   The parents
   The outside community (*e.g.*, the media)
   Other _____

8. My feeling is, (check only one):
   Nothing can be done to improve the school.
   I'm willing to improve the school if techniques are found.

As a result of the survey, we found that the staff believed Westinghouse was an above average or average school (64%) and believed, if techniques could be found, was improvable. While most believed that the greatest impediment to improvement was the principal and administration (37%), some placed responsibility on their colleagues (8%). The staff felt that the principal lacked the techniques necessary to implement change. Most felt that students weren't trying (81%) but that parents were cooperative (63%) if they were contacted.

The survey provided a good starting point to open a discussion on the need to change things at Westinghouse.

4

GETTING STARTED STRATEGIES

There are seven essential steps to getting started in Total Quality. In this chapter, we will discuss each of the steps. On the next page is a list of these steps. We begin here with step 1.

STEP 1. MAKING AN ADMINISTRATIVE COMMITMENT

All of the quality theorists agree that Total Quality will not work unless there is a commitment by management. Deming and Juran insist that at least 85% of the problems in business are caused by management and that 15% or less are caused by the workers.

Teachers and other members of the Westinghouse staff were skeptical and apprehensive about change. According to what teachers were told, every change in education was designed to make their lives easier and was going to solve the problems they faced. And after each wonder cure failed, a new "flavor of the month" was produced. Therefore, the commitment to Total Quality Education must be more than a verbal one.

SEVEN ESSENTIAL STEPS IN GETTING STARTED

Making an Administrative Commitment.

Selecting a Quality Coordinator.

Writing a Mission Statement.

Identifying your Customers and Suppliers.

Involving your Internal and External Customers.

Finding out more about the Process.

Institutionalizing your Process.

The superintendent or principal cannot say to staff, "You go out and do the job and when you have finished, report back to me." The principal or superintendent must act as a general who leads his troops. He or she must be in front of the charge, not in the rear. People involved in Total Quality call this "walking the talk." Deming, in his book, repeatedly talks about a need for "Constancy of Purpose," and this is the first of his "14 Points." The process will not work without it. Total Quality Education will fail without a sincere management commitment to the implementation of change.

The commitment must be visually demonstrated. When we began the process (on January 30, 1991) the principal, Lewis A. Rappaport, stood in front of the faculty and said, "We are a good school. But there are things which are not working. The reason they are not working is because of the process we are using. I am responsible for the process and need your help in changing it. We think we have a way to make the process work better. It is called Total Quality Management. As long as I am principal of this school, we will use Total Quality techniques to address our challenges."

By addressing the faculty in this manner, Mr. Rappaport demonstrated several essential elements needed to make Total Quality Education work. He clearly demonstrated his commitment to making the process work. He asked for faculty support; he took the responsibility for what was not working, and he expressed long-term support for the process. His actions took courage. History books have many stories about generals who wanted the victories but were unwilling or unable to fight the battles. Any educational leader who is unwilling or unable to fight for Total Quality should avoid joining the fray.

STEP 2. SELECTING A QUALITY COORDINATOR

The job of a principal or superintendent is to direct the school or district. We found that adding the task of running the Total Quality Program was too much for the principal. The primary jobs of the principal in the Total Quality process should be to serve as a catalyst for change and as an "enabler" providing the resources, time, and space necessary to enable the process to work. He or she should also serve as a cheerleader, encouraging, both through word and action, the efforts of the Quality Coordinator and the rest of the Quality Team.

Mr. Rappaport found someone who was convinced that Total Quality Management could be transferred to education. The Quality Coordinator selected was also an assistant principal who taught a class and supervised several teachers. The choice had merit because the assistant principal was in contact with teachers, students, parents, the administration, and external customers. Ideally, the Coordinator's position should be full-time so that he or she can deal with all of the issues related to the design and implementation of the process. Our superintendent was asked to give the Quality Coordinator additional released nonteaching time. Due to budgetary concerns, the superintendent was unable to fulfill this request.

We feel that there are a number of attributes that a quality coordinator must possess:

- ◆ He or she must believe in the process and must have an expertise in the philosophy, tools, and techniques of Total Quality.
- ◆ The Quality Coordinator must have the ability to lead people. He or she must see the need and act on it.
- ◆ He or she must have excellent written and oral communication skills and a sense of vision. Internal customers must be convinced that the idea of Total Quality is good and workable.
- ◆ A Quality Coordinator must know how to build consensus. Therefore, he or she must be a conciliator and must engender trust and respect.
- ◆ The coordinator must be able to delegate power and responsibility.

The Quality Coordinator meets frequently with the principal, proposing various courses of action. In addition, it is the quality coordinator's job to:

- ◆ Lead the quality movement in the school.

- Set the direction that the Total Quality Education movement will take (with the guidance of the principal and steering committee).
- Meet with the various customer groups and visitors.
- Do extensive reading.
- Conduct training workshops.
- Establish the vision path and pursue it.
- Serve as the leader of the Quality Steering Committee.
- Maintain an expertise by taking Total Quality workshops and seminars.

The Coordinator position should be full-time. He or she should not take on tasks other than those related to the design and implementation of the process.

STEP 3. WRITING A MISSION STATEMENT

Too frequently, the various members of a school-community view one another as adversaries rather than as members of a single team. A mission statement helps to align often disparate components of a school's organization; it helps to develop a common vision. It provides staff, students, parents, and the external customers a clear vision of the purpose of the school. Without a mission statement, a school lacks direction and frequently causes various customers to work at cross purpose. This resembles a football team with 11 quarterbacks, each with different signals, different objectives and different methods.

If we were to continue to use a football analogy, imagine the schematic diagram on the next page as describing the situation:

A SCHOOL WITHOUT A MISSION STATEMENT

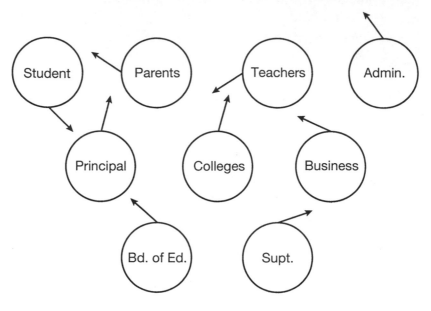

A SCHOOL WITH A MISSION STATEMENT

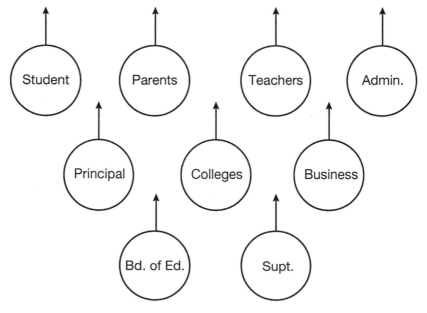

By aligning the forces, a mission statement creates a synergy—that is, a whole greater than the sum of its parts.

The mission statement of Westinghouse High School was written by the staff after much discussion and, occasionally, raised voices. It took 4 months to be written and approved. The mission statement hangs in the classrooms of the school as a constant reminder of what we wish to achieve.

Westinghouse Mission Statement

**The purpose of George Westinghouse
Vocational and Technical High School
is to provide quality vocational,
technical, and academic educational programs
which will maximize each student's
full potential in today's changing
technological society
and prepare students to meet the challenges
of our rapidly changing world.
In an era of intense international competition,
each student
will be prepared to meet the demands of the world
of work, pursue post-secondary education,
and address life's challenges.**

Mission statements should be short and easy to remember. Ours is probably too long, but it demonstrates the cooperative effort made by staff to incorporate all of our beliefs. Given the alternative between a short mission statement and one which represents the larger group, choose the latter.

STEP 4. IDENTIFYING YOUR CUSTOMERS AND SUPPLIERS

If we expect to change the schools we must identify whom the school serves. Like the business community, schools are composed of suppliers and customers and an end product. The product produced in schools should be an educated graduate. Westinghouse's suppliers include elementary and intermediate schools, parents, the teachers, counselors, and administrators in our "feeder schools, and the community. At Westinghouse, we have identified our staff, students, and parents as internal customers. Our external customers are the recipients of our graduates, the colleges and universities, the business community, the military, and the community at large.

The various components of our school may have different suppliers and customers. Our secretaries have different customers than our cafeteria workers. In all probability, they will have different suppliers. It is essential that each group within a school identify its own set of suppliers and customers.

In making decisions, we must take into account our suppliers and customer's needs. Unless we identify who our suppliers and customers are, and what their needs are, we will be unable to satisfy them. Schools must work with both the suppliers and customers in order to produce its product. Traditionally, schools have imposed their demands on the customer and supplier and have alienated them. Instead of telling of customers what we expect of them, now is the time to start asking our customers what *we* must bring to the arena to help them achieve what we both want. Unless and until there is open dialogue, the schools will continue to do what we have always done and get the same results.

STEP 5. INVOLVING YOUR INTERNAL AND EXTERNAL CUSTOMERS

Studies show that as school children grow older parental involvement within the school diminishes. To ask parents to stay involved or to reinvest themselves in high school takes a shift of immense proportions. They must be made to feel that it is their best interests to stay involved with high school student.

To ask students to assist in their own learning and to make suggestions to help others is something unheard of. This process should not be started in the high schools, but rather as soon as the children enter school. Initially, there is great resistance. Motivation for student learning has mainly been extrinsic. Parents and teachers have told students they have to learn. Frequently, this extrinsic motivation has had the opposite effect than it was designed to have.

The last time most business people were in a high school was the day they graduated or the day they attended their child's Open School Day. Obviously, schools have changed since then. Business people should be drawn back into the schools, not only to see the changes that have occurred but because it makes economic sense for the business person as well. Too frequently the businessperson who enters the schools is besieged with requests for money as if that is the only thing that schools need from the business community. By becoming involved with the school, the business person can make suggestions regarding curriculum and the current equipment being used in the workplace.

The college and university customers have a great deal to gain and to share with the high schools. The high schools are suppliers to the higher education establishment. If colleges wish to help raise educational standards of the public schools, they must assume a more active role. The colleges need to recognize that the public schools are both suppliers and customers.

STEP 6. FINDING OUT MORE ABOUT THE PROCESS

When we began our process, we decided to copy ("benchmark," *i.e.*, the identification and copying of the best in the field) from industrial groups who were further along in the Total Quality process then we were. Motorola generously allowed us to attend a "Stalking Six Sigma" workshop. Digital Equipment Company allowed us to sit in with three of their top quality experts. The Marriott Corporation, NYNEX, IBM, and Xerox all willingly supplied Total Quality training.

Total Quality is a "hot" topic generating the formation of networks, consultants, newsletters, videos, and books. The interested individual will not find any difficulty locating material about either Total Quality Management or Total Quality Education.

A bibliography containing the names of books, newsletters, networks, and videos appears in Appendix C. For those about to embark on the journey, we suggest the following initial core of books and videos:

- **Stephen Covey's** *Seven Habits of Highly Effective People* describes the tenants of Total Quality without ever using the name. His latest book, *Principle-Centered Leadership,* links the seven habits to Total Quality.

- **Lloyd Dobbins and Claire Crawford-Mason's** *Quality or Else* is an encyclopedic history of the Total Quality movement. This book is a companion piece to the Deming Library video of the same name.

- Peter Capezio and Debra Morehouse's *Taking The Mystery Out of TQM: A Practical Guide to Total Quality Management* is written in simple language and can be used as a high school text.

- *Quality is Free,* **by Philip R. Crosby,** is a fast reading, easily understood book whose theme is that quality is free, it is the lack of quality which is expensive.

- **GOAL/ QPC's** *Memory Jogger for Education* demonstrates how to use the tools in the educational environment. The **Juran Institute's** *Quality Improvement Pocket Guide* is equally as good. Its limitation is that it does not merely deal with education.

- *Continuous Quality Improvement: A New Look for Education,* a video made jointly by the American Society for Quality Control and the American Association for School Administrators, demonstrates how four school districts and one inner-city school are using Total Quality in education. This short video (23 minutes) shows the many ways that Total Quality can change the nature of schools.

- *Quality in Education: Deming in the Schools* is a part of the Deming Library. The video is made by

CCM Productions which introduced Dr. Deming
to the United States in 1980 in a NBC television
show entitled, "If Japan Can, Why Can't We?"

We suggest establishing a "Quality Library" for those who
wish to delve more deeply and read the numerous books,
articles and view the videos which have appeared. Those
schools with larger budgets may wish to give the key players
a copy of each of these books. These expenditures will be
rapidly amortized with the savings that result after
implementing Total Quality Management.

STEP 7. INSTITUTIONALIZING YOUR PROCESS

Total Quality, whether in industry or education, has been
championed by individuals who see the need to make changes.
When some of those champions left the movement, their
organizations faltered and frequently passed on. In some cases,
the new leader took the attitude that since it didn't happen on
his watch, it didn't happen at all.

Institutionalizing the process is like planting a tree with
deep roots. If a strong wind changes direction, the tree may
bend but the roots will keep the tree upright. Since the average
"life expectancy" of school superintendents is 5 years—3 years
in the inner-cities—institutionalization insures that if the
champion is replaced, other stakeholders will guarantee that the
process continues.

Our quality steering committee represents our
institutionalization of the process. It is made up of volunteer
members of our instructional staff, secretaries, and security
officers. The principal and Quality Coordinator also are
members. During the 1992–93 school year, we broadened the
membership to include students and parents. Meeting once a
week after the school day has ended, this group determines the
next challenge to be addressed. Members of the committee are
unpaid for their efforts and participate out of a desire to make
the process work. Because the group is cross-functional, no
department feels that it has been "left out" of the process.
Members of the committee bring back to their departments
word of what occurred at the weekly meeting. At the same

time, they bring concerns of the departments back to the steering committee. The Quality Steering Committee serves as the school's change agent. Without this dedicated group, the process wouldn't be moving as quickly as it is. We doubt that the process would be moving at all!

The greatest challenge to implementing total quality is the need to effect a culture change. In the educational community, this is extremely difficult. To tell the bureaucracy what they should do to help instruction borders on heresy, with all the images that the word conveys. As in industry, there is a tendency for bureaucrats and middle management to be the most resistant. Both groups feel that they have the most to lose as you share the responsibilities among the various customers.

Teachers did not enter the teaching field to help run the schools. Most of them entered the system in order to effectuate change within the classroom. Even though they are burdened with tasks they never envisioned, they are reluctant to change. For many, the responsibility of helping to run the school is overwhelming when added to the task of teaching and grading papers. But the teachers at Westinghouse, rose to the challenge. They are a hard-working dedicated group of professionals. We are sure that groups similar to ours exist all over our nation. Teaching professionals are just waiting to be asked!

Bringing Total Quality Management into education is like rolling a huge stone up a hill. It is slow, tedious, and hard work. The greatest obstacle is inertia. Once you've overcome it, there are other boulders that will arise. If you can get others to help you push (parents, students, external customers) it makes the task much easier and the job gets done much faster.

The process takes a while to effect a culture change. The time needed for this culture change frequently leads to frustration and cynicism among the staff, the parents, the students, and the bureaucrats. People have to be educated not to expect instant results. Our best advice is to continue to persevere and wear down the resistance. The change is worth the effort. At the same time, do not get too complacent. Remember, once you think you've covered all of the bases, someone will move one of the bases. The Plan-Do-Check-Act cycle is extremely valuable. It makes you use the information that was gathered the last time the cycle was used.

5

GETTING THE STAFF INVOLVED

Teaching is a lonely and unrespected profession. Society continually places additional responsibilities (disguised as curricula) on educators, making the situation worse. Traditional school management treats teachers as mere commodities or expendables, like the thumbtacks and rubberbands it buys.

Pedagogues are called upon to implement plans that they do not necessarily have input into. Supervisors have supplied them with curricula and the Board of Education has supplied them with textbooks. The State Department of Education has supplied them with standardized tests. Teachers frequently see themselves as mere witnesses to learning, more than being the managers of it. When we talk about "self-image" in connection with schools, most often we are talking about student self-image. Maybe we should talk about low self-image in our teaching staff. Teachers represent a highly educated professional group—yet, they and the public state that they are "only a teacher."

School personnel in general, and inner-city teachers in particular, feel as if they are in the middle of a battlefield. They feel that they are being attacked on all sides and their labors are not appreciated or admired by either the outside community or by the people they work for. The leaders of their schools frequently don't appreciate their efforts and treat them like the children they teach. (Until recently teachers in New York City had to "punch" a time clock and they *still* have to bring in doctor's notes when they are absent.) Their cries for assistance are ignored. The buildings that they work in are in disrepair. Their suggestions are viewed as "whining." Many view educators as either babysitters or policemen. Everyone knows what is wrong with education and everyone thinks they know how to fix it. Education is a place where many people think they know more about the job than the people who are working in it. In the past, the answer to the problems in education has been to "fix the teacher."

Teachers represent a skilled, highly-educated, highly-dedicated group of individuals. Many people believe anyone can teach. As professionals, teachers make their job look easy. School districts across the country are having difficulty recruiting staff. If teaching were easy, why is there a 10–15% turnover of teachers every year?

At Westinghouse we felt that we had to demonstrate to our staff that the Taylor Scientific Method of "top-down" organization no longer applied. When people look at the Japanese "miracle" they do not see the Japanese's utilization of their human resources which is a such an inherent part of Total Quality Management. We felt we had to bring the staff into the decisionmaking process so they could make suggestions about running the school and improving the quality of the instructional process at Westinghouse. The staff often know where the flaws in the system lie and should be encouraged to propose improvements in the school.

Like many of us, teachers are not risk-takers. Total Quality Education not only accepts risk-taking, it encourages it. Casey Stengel once said, "I manage good, they just play bad." Teachers and administrators have long viewed each other as adversaries rather than as partners playing on the same team. We felt that we had to blur the line between administration and teachers. As administrators we have to show that our goals are the same as the teachers'. The job of an administrator is to provide the tools and resources so that teachers could do their job well. We believe that the success of a supervisor depends on his or her ability to share responsibility with the workers. You cannot motivate employees into taking action merely by talking to them. A supervisor can create the atmosphere and offer assistance to help teachers achieve the goals for themselves. There has to be a realization that the school administration will not make it without the staff and the staff will not make it without management. Leadership cannot be given to people simply by a word or by a stroke of a pen. Sharing responsibility with employees has to be accompanied by planning, training, and a set of goals. A process needs to be developed so that by working in collaboration we can accomplish shared aims.

New York City has the second highest teacher union membership in the country. In addition, the United Federation of Teachers is one of New York State's most powerful unions. Nearly every teacher and school secretary in New York City is a member of the U.F.T. If the staff and the union rejected the concept, Total Quality Education would not work.

Lewis Rappaport was the 10th principal at Westinghouse in 14 years. The U.F.T. Chapter at Westinghouse had held the school together during the comings and goings of past principals. It remained a constant in a sea of changing administrations, providing stability and continuity for the staff. Many of the school's principals faced great difficulty in dealing with the union. At best, the tenuous relationship was adversarial. It was correctly perceived that the union represented the long-term interests of the staff as principal after principal passed through the doors of Westinghouse on their way to retirement or advancement. Most of the staff liked working in "the House"—whoever might be principal at the moment was of little concern. At the same time, the staff had been told that the latest educational fad would make their teaching life easier. They were skeptical of any administrator who had a plan, and they had every right to be. There had been a 20.79% decrease in staff in 5 years (1989–93) because of Board of Education cuts. We felt that our staff, with more than

20 years experience was skeptical and burned out, but professionally desirous of being challenged.

The rapid turnover of principals, the deteriorating state of the building, the frustration of working for a bureaucracy which didn't listen, and the low pay demoralized not only the staff at Westinghouse, but teachers all over New York City.

All of the Quality theorists agree that training is essential if total quality is to be implemented. Most training in New York City high schools is done by the Assistant Principals of Supervision. They train members of their departments in developing teaching strategies and in classroom management techniques. Monthly faculty meetings deal mainly with administrative items. When schoolwide training meetings have been held, they have dealt with Board of Education mandated topics like HIV/AIDS, "No Guns in School," and Racial Harmony. January 30, 1991, was different. Each school was permitted to develop its own staff development agenda, enabling us to roll out Total Quality Education.

The possibility of staff rejection was great; the school was scheduled to lose 17 members of the teaching staff at the end of the day. (This didn't come about because the United Federation of Teachers came to a last-minute agreement with the Board of Education. The teachers of the City of New York surrendered 3½ days of their own salary to "hire back" those scheduled to be laid-off.) We agreed to start the process because we didn't know if we would ever get another opportunity.

Mr. Rappaport and I prepared an agenda for January 30. At 8:30AM there would be a plenary meeting. At 10AM the staff would choose from one of three workshops. One of the three workshops would be a continuation of the morning Total Quality Management workshop. For the afternoon, we had invited a number of speakers to the school. The speakers would make presentations about non-TQM topics. The only mandatory meeting on Total Quality was the initial session.

After Mr. Rappaport made the commitment to Total Quality, he turned the meeting over to me. I gave the staff a brief history of Total Quality, explaining how the Japanese had used the process to industrialize and how enlightened American businesses were bringing the process back to America. I explained how we needed staff input if we were going to improve the instructional process at Westinghouse. I asked, "How many came into education in order to become wealthy?" After the laughter died down, I asked that each member make a list of the top three reasons they had entered the teaching field. They put their answers on "Post-its" which we then put on the wall in a vertical column. The list included job security, pensions, a short working year, and vacations. The number one item, the item found on almost everyone's list, was that they "wanted to help children." "Imagine if we could find a process which would help us do what we set out to do," I said.

We had devised an experiment to demonstrate that the process was at fault and not the worker. The experiment is called "The Paper Clip Necklace." It is an inexpensive experiment and we believe it demonstrates how workers, by changing the process, can increase productivity.

THE PAPER CLIP NECKLACE EXPERIMENT
MATERIALS NEEDED

- ◆ 20 boxes of paper clips
- ◆ Oak Tag or File Folders
- ◆ Magic Marker
- ◆ Overhead or Newsprint
- ◆ A long work table

OBJECTIVE

- ◆ To make as many paper clip necklaces in 3 minutes as possible.

RUNNING THE EXPERIMENT

To run the experiment you need six volunteers. Each volunteer is given a job.

The first volunteer is the "box opener." The job description of the box opener is to open a box of paper clips and dump the contents on the table. The box opener should also inspect each clip to make sure that it is not defective (broken or bent out of shape).

Volunteer number two is the "counter." The job description of the counter is to count 20 paper clips and to pass the clips to the third person who is the "stringer."

The "stringer" must link the paperclips together to form a chain.

The "inspector," volunteer number four, has the job of counting to make sure that there are exactly 20 paper clips on the chain.

Volunteer number five, the "time keeper," has the job of laying out the chain on the table and keeping time.

Volunteer number six was the "boss." The job of the boss was to encourage workers to do a good job and to hurry the production process.

A sign, made out of file folders, introduced each of the volunteers to the audience. The only mandatory rule was that there wasn't to be any talking between the workers. (Obviously, this would slow down the work process.) The only person who could speak was the boss. Each volunteer could only do the job that had been assigned to him or her and could not assist any other volunteer.

After performing the experiment the first time, a second opportunity was given to the volunteers. In the second round, workers would determine their own jobs and would be allowed to speak and help one another. The only mandate was that no worker could be "laid-off" because of inefficiency.

Invariably, the second time that the experiment is run far more chains are produced. The staff was asked to explain the reasons why. A list was kept on newsprint. This list included:

◆ The workers had become more efficient because they had been allowed to talk, participate, choose their own jobs, and assist each other.

◆ The workers had become more efficient because they had understood the process the second time.

The group concluded that if we change the process to allow more involvement and a greater understanding of what had to be done, we could make our job easier and help students learn.

CHANGING PERSPECTIVES

At 9:50AM we took a coffee break, not knowing how many people would return for the 10AM meeting. At 10AM, 74 people appeared. (The plenary session had 154 people.) We began the meeting by asking how many of them thought that they were doing a quality job. Everyone raised their hands. We asked, "How many of you think that Westinghouse High School was doing a quality job?" Far fewer hands were raised. "How do you explain if everyone is doing a quality job that the school isn't?" Everyone had an answer. We ultimately synthesized the list down to 23:

23 REASONS WHY THE SCHOOL ISN'T DOING A QUALITY JOB

1. Lack of communication between the administration, staff and students.
2. Lack of incentives for students.
3. Student lateness.
4. Poor attendance of students.
5. Grading policy *is not* consistent.
6. Board regulations.
7. The Principal.
8. Large numbers in classes.
9. Negative attitudes between parents, teachers, students, media, administration.
10. Lack of consistency and follow through. Rules are issued and not followed (*e.g.,* hats, beepers, radios, etc.)
11. Lack of clearly defined goals.
12. Lack of cooperation from the administration, teachers, students, parents, and the Board of Education.
13. Students who are disrespectful.
14. Confrontations with students (no back-up by the administration).
15. Missing phone numbers on records. Parents could not be contacted.
16. Lack of values from the students.
17. Rules aren't enforced.
18. Need for stricter penalties.
19. Examples need to be set.
20. Teachers and students feel demoralized.
21. Students feel poorly treated.

22. Selection of students for co-operative program.
23. Lack of time to deal with issues.

Changing Staff Attitudes

The staff was asked to choose the most important inhibitor. They selected the lack of consistency. The administration had established a rule banning students from wearing hats and carrying personal radios ("Walkman" type) and had failed to enforce these and other rules. The rule regarding hat wearing had been established because several visitors (external customers) to the building had made comments about this. We felt that students wouldn't go on job or college interviews wearing a hat and that this policy had implications beyond the school. Students wearing radios failed to pay attention in class and presented a hazard in laboratories while working on machinery.

We distributed an action plan to our staff and asked them to help complete it. They determined that any student wearing a hat or using a radio would have it confiscated. The administration would be responsible for hats and radios in the halls and cafeteria. Classroom teachers would confiscate hats and radios in the classroom. Any teacher seeing the Principal or an Assistant Principal failing to enforce this rule could bring the matter to the Principal's attention. If a teacher permitted the wearing of hats or the use of radios in his or her classroom, they would receive a verbal warning from an Assistant Principal or the Principal. A student's parents would have to come to school in order to retrieve the confiscated hat or radio. We selected Monday, February 14, to begin implementation of this new policy.

We had planned to end the workshop on this note. As the lunch break approached, teachers asked to address the other 22 items. We informed them that we were unable to complete the task in the time allotted and that we would get back to them when we would go on to the other items. Several staff members said that if the administration believed that teachers were customers, we should listen to our customer's request for another workshop. Having been caught on our own petard, we agreed to give another workshop after the lunch break.

During the lunch break, Mr. Rappaport and I attempted to develop a strategy for the afternoon. Word had spread during the lunch break about this new attitude. When we reconvened there were 87 members of the staff in our audience. (One invited guest speaker had seven people in his audience.) We placed on the chalkboard a list of seven inhibitors (the Principal, the rest of the administration, teachers, parents, students, the Board of Education, and the media). The staff members were requested to select one of the inhibitors and to form into a team. They were given "Post-its" and were told to brainstorm how the inhibitor would attempt to stop the implementation of the process and what action the team could recommend to stop the inhibitor. For the first time in a long while, the Principal, the administration, teachers, secretaries, and security officers exchanged views without regard to license or title or department. A dialogue developed. Instead of talking about the day-to-day job of classroom teaching we were attempting to deal with some of the challenges that we faced as a school. When the day came to an end at 2:15PM, several people sat around continuing to discuss the actions necessary to make the process work.

DEMONSTRATING COMMITMENT—THE FIRST CHALLENGE: HATS AND RADIOS

We spent many hours developing a strategy to deal with the hat and radio situation. We had been given a mandate—an important one—because if we failed to deliver on this item we could never convince the staff that we would be able to deliver on anything else. On the first day of Spring Term, Mr. Rappaport stood at the front door with a microphone and announced to all students that effective February 14 all hats and radios worn in the building would be confiscated. Large signs were posted all over the building. Teachers were asked to make announcements in each class. The public address system spewed out the message. A group of administrators stood at the entrance handing out slips of paper, every day for 1 week, advising students of the new policy. The announcement went out over our 24 hour telephone "hotline." It was announced at the monthly Parent Teachers' Association meeting. We believed that these actions would insure a saturation of the student population and would demonstrate to the faculty that we were serious about their concern.

On February 14, we began confiscating hats and radios. Mr. Rappaport went on the public address system and announced, "I want to thank the 1500 students who didn't wear their hat or radio. To the 211 students whose hat or radio we confiscated, your parent will have to pick it up." On Tuesday, he announced, "I want to thank the 1600 students who didn't wear their hat or radio. To the 117 students whose hat or radio we confiscated, your parent will have to pick it up." On Wednesday, he announced, "Our message is getting across, I want to thank the 1600 students who didn't wear their hat or radio. To the 87 students whose hat or radio we confiscated, your parent will have to pick it up." By Friday, we had reduced the number of confiscated hats or radios to 37. We had established a policy and enforced it. We had created a major policy shift. Many staff members reluctantly agreed that we were doing something. One skeptic, who had said to me on January 30 that the new policy would not work, came by and apologized.

DEMONSTRATING COMMITMENT—THE SECOND CHALLENGE: STUDENTS WHO HAD FAILED EVERY CLASS

For our next challenge we chose students who had failed every single class (100% failure) for the Fall 1991 term. Our computer printout indicated that there were 151 students, in all grades, who had failed every single class. Volunteer members of the staff, using a cause and effect diagram, investigated the root causes of these student failings. They did an oral survey of some of these students. Guidance counselors interviewed some of the parents.

Then we developed an action plan. Our guidance counselors were to interview all of the parents and students from this group and to learn the reasons for the failures. It was suggested to some of these students that they take fewer classes so that they could concentrate their energies on a smaller number of classes. Some parents informed us that they didn't know that failure was unacceptable because their children had been promoted even after they had failed classes in the lower grades. Many students said they needed tutoring. They couldn't stay late due to work obligations or the need for them to take care of younger siblings. One dedicated English teacher created the "Lunch and Learn" program. "Lunch and Learn" provides tutoring when students have lunch. By June 1991, 6 months later, of the original 151 students only 11 still had failed every class. Some of the failing students had transferred to other schools. We also did not take a count of how many had failed every class but one. By June, we had 110 new "100% failures" and so the process began again.

We now use the "Lunch and Learn" Program to assist any student who needs help in mastering material. In June of 1993, we were informed that 62 students had been serviced by "Lunch and Learn" in eight academic and technical areas, and 71% of these students passed the classes for which they received tutoring.

DEMONSTRATING COMMITMENT—THE THIRD CHALLENGE: CUTTING THE "CUTTING" RATE

The "cutting" rate, students not going to classes, at Westinghouse, like many schools is horrendous. Not only do these students not go to class but they wander through the building disrupting instruction. Our next challenge was to address this problem. By using the tools (action plan, cause and effect diagram, and check lists) provided by the process, we were able to reduce cutting by 39.9% in a 6-week period.

THE QUALITY STEERING COMMITTEE

By now, the process had taken a life of its own. It was reducing Mr. Rappaport and my ability to to run the school and supervise instruction. By June of 1991 we became aware of the need to "broaden the circle"—to involve more people. We were concerned that if the Principal or the Quality Coordinator left, the process would die. We developed a plan to create a "Quality Steering Committee." We designed the Steering Committee as a means of institutionalizing the process. The purpose of the Steering Committee is to:

- Share some of the responsibility of running Total Quality Management
- Institutionalize the process
- Serve as the school's change agent
- Monitor the activities of the Quality Coordinator
- Evaluate the activities of the school
- Support and encourage the individual and committee efforts implementing the quality improvement process
- Serve as a sounding board for administration proposals
- Bring back to their constituencies and departments the decisions of the committee
- Bring to the committee the concerns of departmental members.

We wanted the committee to be cross-functional. That is, it had to have members from every faculty customer group in the school. The committee is representative of all parts of the school community including administrators, teachers, parents, secretaries, students, guidance counselors, and non-pedagogical staff and meets once a week for at least an hour after school ends. Staff members do not get paid. They give up their personal time to insure the process works. The meetings are informal and our decisions are reached by consensus. The Principal and Quality Coordinator are permanent members of the committee. The Chapter Chairperson of the United Federation of Teachers is encouraged to attend. The committee serves in the leadership role of the quality improvement process. It decides which issues of concern should be addressed next, and tries to come up with solutions. The process helps the staff devise solutions.

FOLLOWING THROUGH

Teaching is done in isolation. Once a teacher enters the classroom and closes the door, he or she is alone. In addition, teachers rarely discuss their teaching techniques with colleagues. Real and artificial barriers exist in high schools. Departmental "turf" has discouraged cooperation. Total Quality Education has encouraged us to have English and Social Studies interdepartmental meetings to discuss joint concerns, like writing. In English literature classes, students are reading material which complements their Social Studies lessons. In a pilot program, English teachers are grading Social Studies papers for grammar, punctuation, and spelling, while the Social Studies teachers grade the papers for the content's historical correctness. It is a "win-win" situation for everyone involved. Students have to do one very good paper instead of two mediocre ones. English and Social Studies teachers are more comfortable grading papers in their own field.

We have started a *Total Quality Newsletter* in addition to our two weekly bulletins, *The Grapevine* and *Weekly Calendar*. The newsletter identifies what items the Quality Steering Committee is addressing. In addition, it has supplied new staff members with a history of Total Quality Education at Westinghouse. It has helped us to address the staff's concern about a lack of communication.

In order to get suggestions from the staff, we have borrowed an idea from the Marriott Corporation. Any staff member making a suggestion by putting it into the Quality letterbox, receives a thank you letter within 24 hours of receipt. The letter has a "Q-tip" attached to it so as to thank the person for the quality tip provided. The suggestion is then passed on to the Quality Steering committee for disposition.

Two senior teachers in our vocational and technical department have redesigned our freshman program. As in most high schools, Westinghouse has more dropouts from its entering class than any other. Our Apprentice Training Program pairs an entering freshman with a senior mentor. For 10 weeks freshmen are assigned to seniors in shop classes. A freshman works side by side with a senior who guides the freshman through class experiments. Freshmen learn 9th and 10th year skills, and the senior gets leadership responsibilities. (An extra 45 minutes has been added to the senior program to provide them with increased instruction.) Teachers say there is less boredom in the class, thus less disruption and a lot more focus on work. As a result of the pilot year, 28 freshmen in the program received a grade of 85 or better. Of an equal number of those not in the program, 14 received a grade of 85 or better. Attendance of those in the sample group was higher than for those not in the program. The pilot program was so successful that every shop teacher has joined the program.

The Apprentice Training Program forms a new paradigm of learning. It makes each pupil both a teacher and a student. Instead of one teacher teaching a class of 28 students, there are 14 senior mentors teaching 14 freshmen students without an increase in costs. Senior students reinforce their own learning and serve as a guide and coach for a junior member of the school. Both the coach and the student learn from each other. Self-esteem is also raised. Freshmen have someone in the school to identify with—a student who has succeeded, someone who will graduate soon. "The teacher" no longer sits in front of the class—he or she sits beside you. Seniors are given an extra 45 minutes of instruction so as to increase their own material. We also found that our seniors are able to teach faster, so we have added two additional units to the freshman curriculum. Team formation is taking place in the classroom.

The three trade departments have held joint meetings to coordinate ordering of supplies, and instructional problems which they jointly share. They are investigating additional techniques to provide greater communication between them.

The school lacks the ability to do much teacher training. One day a month there is a mandatory faculty meeting. According to the teacher union contract, for 45 minutes the principal holds a meeting with teachers to discuss upcoming events. In most schools, the principal distributes a written agenda and then proceeds to expand on its contents. We felt that this was a missed opportunity to do total quality training. Mr. Rappaport now begins most meetings by asking if there are any questions regarding the written agenda which was expanded to provide explanations. If there aren't any questions, we proceed to the professional topic which is about the further implementation of quality. In this way, our professional topic now takes 35 minutes and the administrative items take 10 minutes. Previously, it had been the reverse.

A number of teachers criticized the lack of consistency in grading and grading standards. Over a 5 month period, the

Steering Committee, meeting weekly, developed a contract which is binding on parents, students, and staff. For the next 4 months, the staff, a group of students, and the Parents Teachers Association made suggestions and modifications. Some of the discussions were heated. In June 1992, we took a vote of the school staff. Over 70% approved the contract. In September 1992, the contract went into effect. The contract is reproduced beginning on the next page.

By issuing a set of rules, we have provided several features:

◆ There aren't any hidden agendas. The contract represents an effort to notify our internal customers what is expected of each of them. School rules are clearly stated for staff, students, and parents. The rules are clearly posted and are sent home to parents at the beginning of the school year.

◆ The rules are consistent. A teacher or department cannot change, alter, or modify the terms of the school contract. The principal has clearly stated that he will support any teacher who, by using the contract, arrives at a grade.

◆ We have requested and received staff, student, and parent input into the design and terms of the contract.

Using the Shewart Cycle, we reviewed the contract before imposing it in the 1993–94 school term. We asked for and received comments from parents, students, and staff. Those changes have been implemented. We will continue to make changes as frequently as necessary.

GEORGE WESTINGHOUSE VOCATIONAL AND TECHNICAL HIGH SCHOOL CONTRACT

This contract states what is expected of you at Westinghouse Vocational & Technical High School. It will assist you in successfully completing courses. Just follow a few simple rules.

1. GRADES

Grades are cumulative. **They are based on the entire term's performance.** Passing tests and/or shop assignments, good attendance, **punctuality**, satisfactory homework, class and shop participation are all factors in determining your grade. Passing tests and/or *class or* shop assignments is the most important of these.

2. ATTENDANCE

School attendance rules will be strictly enforced.

Absences: A student with two (2) unexcused absences in a marking period or five (5) for the term cannot receive a grade higher than 65. If you exceed the total number of unexcused absences allowed for each marking period or for the term, you may fail. Examples of **excused** absences are a medical excuse, a parental note including a daytime phone number, a court appearance, a quarantine notice, etc. *An absence note will only be accepted on the day the student returns.*

Cutting: **A cut is an unexcused absence.** *A student out of the class room without permission is cutting.*

Lateness: Two latenesses equal one **unexcused** absence. All students reporting after 10 o'clock must report to the Assistant Principal-Guidance (Pupil Personnel Services in Room 152).

3. PREPARATION

Each student is expected to bring *working* pencils and pens to class and basic assigned tools for the shops and maintain a section of their notebook with paper for each subject's work. If you are absent, it is your responsibility to get the missing notes and written material and to make up all missed work. Being unprepared will affect your grade.

4. CLASS PARTICIPATION AND SHOP/ CLASSWORK

This is an important part of your grade. Class participation shows your interest. Students should feel free to express their opinions and ideas by speaking in class *when called on* and not interrupting other students. You should be attentive and copy any notes from the chalkboard. *Shop and classwork,* time on task, and class participation are required to earn credit toward your report card grades.

5. HOMEWORK

Homework will be assigned regularly and is an indication of student effort. *There will be at least 10 graded homeworks per marking period returned to students.* It will be collected and checked. If done properly, it will help you participate in class and act as a study guide for exams. If you are absent, you must make up any missed homework within a reasonable time (to be determined by the subject teacher). If you were present *or unexcused,* make up assignments *may* not be accepted.

6. EXAMS

There will be at least three (3) *previously* announced full-period tests. If you miss an exam, you will not be given an opportunity for a make-up without a note from a doctor or a parent (with a daytime phone number included).

7. DECORUM

Wearing of hats, or non-religious headwear by males or females, eating or drinking in class, carrying a Walkman type radio or beeper, chewing gum, writing on desks or walls, etc., or using abusive language *or physical abuse* will not be permitted. *Compliance with shop safety rules is mandatory.* Your classroom behavior is an indication of your readiness and willingness to learn.

EACH SUBJECT AREA MAY ISSUE ADDITIONAL RULES

I HAVE READ AND UNDERSTOOD WHAT IS EXPECTED OF ME IN MY CLASSES.

Student's Name_____Signature_____

Parent's Signature_____Date_____

Emergency Phone #_____

We have developed a questionnaire, reproduced beginning on the next page, for our staff regarding the contract.
This questionaire will be distributed to the staff toward the end of the 1993–94 school year and will be used to formulate further changes in the contract.

During the school year 1992–93, we added students and parents to the Steering Committee. The meetings are now held in the largest room in the school, the school library. Because of the increased size, we have developed five task forces to deal with the challenges we face. Each task force has been applying the various tools in dealing with their situations. Once a month, the task forces report back to the committee as a whole. They make requests for additional time, personnel, or advice. Staff requests to join the committee have increased and members are added regularly. The principal and quality coordinator have occasionally been unable to attend because of other commitments. The committee has been able to function without their presence.

Recently, a math teacher with a background in statistics has agreed to provide training in the use of the tools to the committee. She has agreed to serve, unpaid, as the Statistical Coordinator and the Coordinator of the Steering Committe for the school.

We have encouraged active participation by staff. One method of doing this is by asking for and acknowledging staff suggestions. We have created a "Quality" mailbox. Any staff member who wishes to make a suggestion can do so by merely putting that suggestion in the Quality mailbox. By sharing the decisionmaking responsibilities of the school, we have gained a greater commitment and involvement from the staff in the running of the school.

	Strongly Agree	Agree	Disagree	Strongly Disagree
1. I felt that the students were more concerned with their grades.				
2. I felt that the students were more concerned with their attendance.				
3. I felt that the students were more concerned with their preparation				
4. I felt that the students were more concerned with their participation.				
5. I felt that the students were more concerned with their homework.				
6. I felt that the students were more concerned with their examinations.				
7. I felt that the students were more concerned with their decorum.				

	Strongly Agree	Agree	Disagree	Strongly Disagree
8. I felt that the contract provided a more consistent implementation of School rules and regulations.				
9. I saw a change in student behavior in the classroom.				
10. Student work and behavior have improved as a result of the contract.				
11. The contract has strengthened my pride and the joy I feel about work.				
12. Staff members thoroughly understand the need to enforce all provisions of the contract.				
13. I need further clarification of the contract.				

Some of our staff failed to understand their role regarding their job and their supplier's needs and requirements and the requirements of their customer. We developed the chart that appears on the next page to explain the relationships.

Our fundamental belief holds that we must have high expectations for our students and must provide the necessary resources so that they can achieve those levels. This requires that the role of teachers should change as well. Teachers must learn to leave the role of "teller" (through lecturing) and assume the role of facilitator. Teachers have to be taught how to lead students to knowledge. For those staff members who have spent their entire educational career lecturing to their students, this is a difficult thing to change.

We have a long way to go. We do not have the support of *all* of our staff and probably never will. Some are skeptical. Many times when we have taken one step forward, the Board of Education's budget cuts have forced us to take two steps back. The challenges have not only been caused by budget cuts and outside forces, we have internal inhibitors. We hear phrases like

"I was here before you. I will be here after you leave."

"I have one foot out the door."

"It will never work."

"Schools are different."

"We're not a factory. We're not a business."

"We're dealing with kids here."

"The students, parents, fellow teachers, and administrators have gotten worse."

"We'll never overcome our students problems."

Many teachers are content with the status quo. It is amazing that people who will not accept the lack of quality in their personal lives are so ready to accept it in their professional life.

UNDERSTANDING THE WORK PROCESS

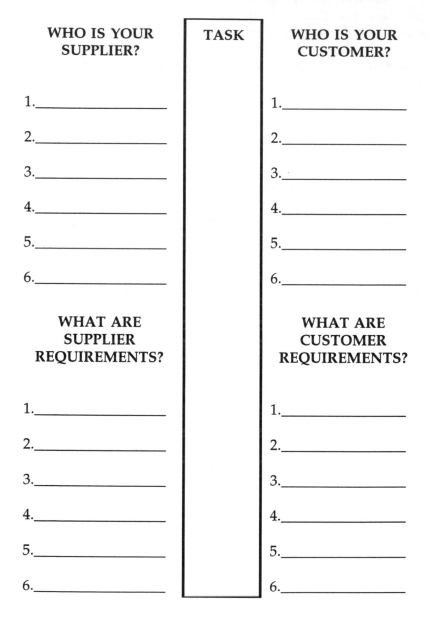

WHO IS YOUR SUPPLIER?

1._____

2._____

3._____

4._____

5._____

6._____

TASK

WHO IS YOUR CUSTOMER?

1._____

2._____

3._____

4._____

5._____

6._____

WHAT ARE SUPPLIER REQUIREMENTS?

1._____

2._____

3._____

4._____

5._____

6._____

WHAT ARE CUSTOMER REQUIREMENTS?

1._____

2._____

3._____

4._____

5._____

6._____

The reluctance to change has not only come from the teaching staff. Some administrators and supervisors have been reluctant to change. They feel that the change will result in their loss of control and power. Efforts have been taken, through training, to overcome these fears. The principal has asked that each of the administrators become a member of the Quality Steering Committee. Each Cabinet Meeting (a monthly meeting held by the principal with the members of his administration) includes a segment about the quality efforts. Skepticism still exists within the staff, but every time we have used the process with success, more staff has joined with us.

Old habits are difficult to break. There is a tendency to slip; to revert to our old ways of doing things. There is a constant need to renew our new beliefs. We need to constantly train our staff less they fall back into bad habits. We have to give them the skills to solve the classroom problems they face. They must be trained to teach students how to work on teams. We must provide them with opportunities to put those skills to immediate use.

What we have to come to realize is that each member of the staff is a part of our quality system and that each has a role in helping improve the school. We have formed a new relationship with the teacher's union. We have come to gain an understanding and appreciation of each other's role and how we can mutually help our students.

6

GETTING THE PARENTS TO BUY IN

Total Quality teaches us to recognize that parents are one of our customers and therefore constitutes a critical element in school improvement. We must identify our parents' expectations and then attempt to satisfy them.

Parents are the first teachers of their children, instilling values, teaching children how to talk, write, count, and learn the alphabet. We felt that since they sent their most prized possession to school, they would be willing to assist educators and act as extended agents of the school in the home. Their involvement could serve to encourage a student's efforts and accomplishments. With this premise in mind, we felt we had to involve parents in the paradigm shift. Since a significant portion of our parents had failed to finish school themselves, our challenge was how to bring parents into accepting a place in the school.

Statistics show that as a child goes through the school system, parental involvement diminishes. There are many possible reasons for this:

♦ There are younger children at home who may need additional attention.

♦ Single-parent and double-working parents do not have time to visit schools at the end of their busy work day.

♦ Many parents assume that as a child matures into the teenage years, the child should assume the responsibility of successfully completing school.

♦ School professionals have not encouraged parental involvement.

When we came to Westinghouse 7 years ago, the Parents Teachers Association membership consisted of 10–12 parents. The first meetings of the year started with high parent attendance. As the year went on, attendance fell. Frequently, the monthly meetings had more staff in attendance than parents. We felt we needed to create an effective outreach to our parents.

In New York City, parent-teacher meetings are scheduled by the principal in consultation with the president of the Parents Teachers Association. The agenda is worked out in the same manner. Most frequently the agenda is the educator's agenda. When parents do not come to meetings, the typical response from an educator is, "They are obviously not interested in their children."

We decided to focus on parents as internal customers and ask them, rather then tell them, what to do. It was time to ask them what they needed to be able to assist in the education of their children instead of telling them what they had to do. We knew from previous experience that the largest Parents Teachers Association meeting was the first one. The parents of our new students wanted to see the school for the first time, and the parents of our upper class students wanted to learn about the new changes that were planned.

We wanted to initiate the parental involvement component with the September 1992 meeting. A number of the school's administrators, supervisors, and volunteer teachers, aided by the President of the Parents Teachers Association, began by using some of the tools to increase parental attendance at this first meeting. We started brainstorming why parents didn't attend. Using a fishbone diagram, we identified the causes of low attendance at Parents Teachers meetings. We used a Pareto Chart to identify and focus on "the vital few" reasons. An action plan allowed us to place responsibility with a number of individuals and helped us identify the resources that were needed. We felt that meetings weren't announced in a timely manner and that a failure to properly communicate the date, time, and purpose of the meetings contributed to low attendance.

As a result, we distributed announcements about the meeting to students as they left the building. Using the school's computer, we telephoned parents at home during the evening and weekend hours, informing them about the meeting and the need for them to attend. The Parents Teachers Association paid for a mailing of notices to all of the parents.

One hundred sixteen parents and students showed for the meeting. It was the largest turnout of parents in memory. The meeting started with a brief history of Total Quality. We informed the parents that we felt that Total Quality would be the best means of helping their children. We wanted to know who our customers were so we distributed a survey for them to complete.

SURVEYING OUR PARENTS

Our survey was not scientific and had several flaws. One obvious flaw was that it was taken only by those parents who came to the meeting. Although the parents who attended did not represent a random sample of our total population, we felt, based on other information, they represented the socio/economic make-up of the school. We cannot, with certainty, assume that those who came were truly representative of all of our parents.

We believed that we would increase attendance if we scheduled meetings at the time and day when most parents said they would attend. In addition, our survey attempted to verify some of the information supplied by the Board of Education. We also desired to gather new data on meeting times and agenda items. The survey we used begins on the next page.

WESTINGHOUSE PARENTS SURVEY

Will you please take a few moments and answer this survey? We are attempting to gather information so that we can better aid your child to progress in this school.

IT IS NOT NECESSARY TO PUT YOUR NAME ON THIS SHEET. PLEASE ANSWER THIS AS HONESTLY AS POSSIBLE.

Please return this sheet where you received it. Leave it at the front desk.

1. Are you:
   Single
   Separated
   Married
   Divorced
   Widowed

2. How many children do you have?
   1
   2
   3
   4
   5 or more

3. What is the highest level of *your* education?
   Never finished elementary school
   Never finished high school
   High School graduate
   College graduate
   Post graduate degrees

4. What is the highest level of *your husband's/wife's* education?
   Never finished elementary school
   Never finished high school
   High School graduate
   College Graduate
   Post graduate degrees

5. What is your family income?
   $10,000–$20,000 a year
   $20,000–$25,000 a year
   $25,000–$35,000 a year
   $35,000–$50,000
   $50,000–$100,000
   Over $100,000

6. I would like the following topics discussed at PTA meetings. (Check all that apply.)
   Career training for parents
   Employment possibilities for my child
   College Opportunities for my child.
   How I can help my child in school.
   Raising children.
   Graduation requirements
   Other_____

7. When is the best *time* for you to attend PTA meetings? (Choose one)
   In the morning (8AM–12 NOON)
   Afternoons (1PM–4PM)
   Evening _____5PM   _____6PM   _____6:30PM
           _____7PM   _____7:30PM   _____8PM
           _____8:30PM

8. When is the best *day* for you to attend PTA meetings? (Circle one)
   Monday   Tuesday   Wednesday   Thursday   Friday
       Saturday Morning   Saturday Afternoon
       Sunday Morning   Sunday Afternoon

We didn't know what kind of responses we would receive from the group. We felt that they might consider some of the questions too personal or they wouldn't answer any of the questions. After we collected the survey we asked the parents for their reaction. Most did not have any problem with the questions. They offered suggestions to improve our survey. They suggested questions that we hadn't thought about (*e.g.*, "Why didn't you ask what foreign languages are spoken at home? This could help you provide additional services to the children that you serve.") We informed them that we would compile the results and report the results at the next meeting.

WHAT WE DISCOVERED ABOUT OUR PARENTS

Based on those parents who attended this 1992 meeting, we found that 27% of our parents are single, 7% are divorced, 19% are separated, .5% are widowed, and 46% are married. Most of our parents have two or more children: 13½% have one child; 28.8% have two children; 29.7% have three children; 18% have four children; and 9.9% have five or more children.

We also found that 2% of our parents had not finished elementary school; 19¾% had not completed high school; 58% graduated from high school; almost 15% have a college degree; and 4% have a post-graduate college degree.

Regarding spouse's education, less than 2% had not finished elementary school; slightly over 37½% had never finished high school; 58% had graduated from high school; and 2% had college degrees.

Slightly less than one half of our parents earn between $10,000 and $20,000; 18% earn between $20,000 and $25,000; 19% earn between $25,000 and $35,000; almost 13% earn between $35,000 and $50,000; and less than 1% earns over $50,000.

What did the parents want discussed at the meetings? Most wanted to discuss college opportunities for their children, followed closely by employment possibilities for their children, and how they could help their child in school. Some (15%) wanted to know graduation requirements. The item that the parents wanted to discuss least was advice on how to raise their children.

The parents wanted meetings held either on Wednesday or Thursday and they wanted the meetings to start at 6:30PM. We were surprised that the third choice of meeting time was between 1–4PM. When we asked why they said that they wanted to see their child at work in the school.

WHAT WE LEARNED FROM THE SURVEY

What did we learn as a result of the survey? We formed a portrait of our customer. We believe that our "typical"

Westinghouse family is composed of one adult with two or three children who graduated from high school and is earning between $10,000 and $20,000 a year. We plan to distribute the survey every year to sample our current parent population. (Nineteen percent of our parents had not answered questions dealing with family income, even though they answered all of the other questions.)

The survey confirmed many of our assumptions and contradicted others. We assumed we knew who our parents were and what they wanted. We assumed that they wanted assistance in raising their children. We assumed that parents would come for meetings when we, the educators, told them to come. Our assumptions were incorrect. Our parents indicated their desire to help us help their children.

WHAT CHANGED AS A RESULT OF THE SURVEY

Based on the survey results, we made several changes in our meeting schedule. To start, Mr. Rappaport moved the time of the meetings to 6:30 in the evening from 6 o'clock and started holding some meetings on Thursday. (We had always held P.T.A. meetings on Wednesday.) The agenda began to reflect parents' concerns and wants. Teachers and other staff members began attending the parents meetings regularly. The parents asked them to join and formed a Parents Teachers Association. Membership in the Parents Teachers Association has grown. In the school year 1991–92, we had 211 paid members of our PTA

Parents have begun to accept an active role in the school. The parents suggested, as a result of the first Rodney King trial, to hold a "Family Night." Staff, parents, and students would prepare food, sing songs, and exchange stories about heritage. The largest room in the school is the school library, with seating for 150 people. We had planned to hold Family Night in the library, not knowing how many people would come. The event grew larger than the capacity of the library and we had to move the event to the student cafeteria (capacity 500). In 1993, we held the Second Annual Family Night in the YMCA. Awards were given to staff and to parents who have helped further our new culture. The PTA plans to hold Family Night as an annual event.

In 1992, the parents decided to formalize their PTA rules and wrote their by-laws. For the first time in recent memory, parents are now competing for Parents Teachers Association offices. They have begun to invite their own speakers to their meetings.

Parents have asked to and are assisting in developing new surveys to learn more about our parents, students, and learning. One of the surveys prepared with the parents' help begins on page 107.

This survey was distributed at a recent Parent Teachers Association meeting. As a result of the surveys completed by those who attended the meeting and responded, we determined that most students study at least an hour a day at home. Like most students in the country, they listen to radio, TV, or the stereo while doing homework (68%). Most parents do not check their child's homework (62%) but they do review the results of tests (68%). Almost 70% of our parents see all six report cards. Over 30% of our parents do not check their child's work because the child doesn't show them any work. We are using the results of this survey to educate the parents on Open School Day on how to check student work, homework, and tests.

In order to involve our parents more deeply, we have asked them to make a commitment to Westinghouse and their children. A Westinghouse Quality Parent Contract has been developed and is distributed at the initial Parents Teachers Association Meeting in September. The contract is reprinted on the page 109.

In return, our parents have asked for greater communication between us. Westinghouse has a term which is divided into three 6-week marking periods. At the end of the marking period teachers place grades on computer sheets. In 7 business days, the computer generates a report card. By the time a parent sees the report card almost one-half of the term has passed—generally too late to change a child's errant behavior. Some students do not bring home their report card.

PARENT SURVEY
Regarding Homework and Tests

Will you please take a few moments and answer this survey? We are attempting to gather information so that we can better aid your child to progress in this school.

IT IS NOT NECESSARY TO PUT YOUR NAME ON THIS SHEET. PLEASE ANSWER THIS AS HONESTLY AS POSSIBLE.

Please return this sheet where you received it or leave it at the front desk as you leave the building.

1. How much time does it take your child to do homework? *(Circle any answer)*

½ hour a day
1 hour a day
More than 2 hours a day
I don't know
My child does not receive homework.
(If you choose this response go to question #5)

2. Does your child do homework while watching television, listening to the radio or stereo, or eating? Yes   No

3. Where does your child do homework? *(Circle all which apply)*

At home
In his or her room
In kitchen
In living room
Somewhere else
Out of house
In library
In school
On the way to or from school
I don't know

4. What time does your child do homework? *(Circle all which apply)*

Morning
Afternoon
Evening

5. **Do you check your child's homework?**   Yes   No

6. **Does your child study for tests?**

Yes

No

   (If your child does not study for tests skip to Question #11)

7. **How long does your child study?** *(TOTAL TIME)*

Less than ½ hour

½ hour

1 hour

2 hours

8. **Where does your child study?** *(Circle all which apply)*

At home

In his or her room

In kitchen

In living room

Somewhere else

Out of house

In library

In school

On the way to or from school

I don't know

9. **Does your child watch television, listen to radio or stereo, eat while studying?**   Yes   No

10. **What time does your child study?**

Morning

Afternoon

Evening

11. **Do you review the results of your child's tests?** *(Circle one answer)*

Yes   No   Occasionally

12.   **We issue 6 report cards a school year. How many do you see?** *(Circle one answer)*

a. 6   c. 4   e. 2   g. 0

b. 5   d. 3   f. 1

13. **If you don't check your child's homework, studying, report cards, why not?**

a. My child doesn't show me any school work.

b. I'm too tired at the end of my day.
c. I'm not interested in my child's work.
d. I have too many other obligations.
e. Other_____

14. Does your child work after school?

Yes

No *(If you have circled this answer you have completed the survey. Thank you!)*

15. Please circle all of the reasons why your child works:

The family needs the money
My child wishes to work
We are saving money for my child's education

Westinghouse Quality Parent Contract

I, as a parent, agree to the following conditions:

1. I pledge that I will attend at least 6 PTA meetings.
2. I pledge that I will regularly check my child's homework.
3. I pledge that I will regularly check my child's tests.
4. I pledge that I will check my child's report card when issued. (6 times a year)
5. I pledge that my child will get a good night's sleep.
6. I pledge that my child will arrive at school on time.
7. I pledge that my child will have a place at home to study.
8. I pledge that I will talk about school with my child on a daily basis.
9. I pledge that I will help my child with homework.
10. I pledge that I will read with my child.
11. I pledge that I will talk to my child's teachers.

_____   _____
Parent's Name   Date

_____   _____
Name of Student   Phone Numbers
                                 (Home-Business)

A number of teachers are currently piloting a "weekly" report card. Students are asked to give themselves a weekly grade and to plot it on a graph. This allows a visual representation of the progress a student makes from week to week. (A grade of 65 is passing.) If a student drops below the heavy line, they and their parents become aware of the need for increased effort. The teacher initials the grade if it falls within the parameter that the teacher believes is correct. If not, the teacher meets briefly with the student and they mutually agree on a grade. The plotting of the grade allows a visual image and demonstrates continuous improvement (or lack of it). Once a parent agrees that their child will be responsible for bringing home the weekly report card, we issue the weekly report card, an illustration of which appears on the next page.

A space at the bottom allows the parent to sign weekly. This report card has allowed a more immediate "feedback" to both parent and student. This feedback keeps the parents informed early enough in the term to make a difference. Students now feel that they have a say in their grades. Teachers report that some students have graded themselves more harshly than the teacher might have. Parents are receiving immediate information and are able to act accordingly.

Another form of communication is a letter to parents informing them of the excellent progress that their child is making. All too often the only contact that a parent has with a school is when their child is not doing well. Imagine receiving a letter like this:

Date:_____

To the parents of _____

I have just been informed that you child received over an 85 in _____. You and (s)he are to be congratulated on the performance in that class.

Speaking on behalf of the principal, we are as proud of your child in this achievement as you are.

Thank you for sending your child to our school!

Sincerely,

_____   _____
Subject Teacher   Assistant Principal

GEORGE WESTINGHOUSE VOCATIONAL HIGH SCHOOL
STUDENTS WEEKLY REPORT CARD

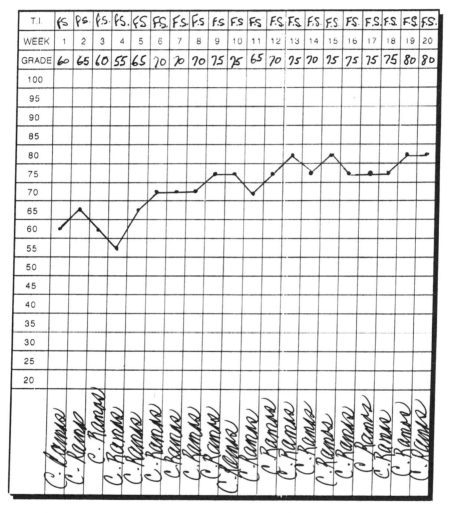

T.I.	F.S	P.S.	P.S.	F.S.	F.S	F.S.	F.S.	F.S	F.S	F.S	F.S	F.S.	F.S.	F.S.	F.S.	F.S.	F.S.	F.S.	F.S.	F.S.
WEEK	1	2	3	4	5	6	7	8	9	10	11	12	13	14	15	16	17	18	19	20
GRADE	60	65	60	55	65	70	70	70	75	75	65	70	75	70	75	75	75	75	80	80
100																				
95																				
90																				
85																				
80																				
75																				
70																				
65																				
60																				
55																				
50																				
45																				
40																				
35																				
30																				
25																				
20																				

American History 2

SUBJECT

Brenda Ramos

STUDENT'S NAME

We are attempting to open new areas of communication with the parents. Surveys will be sent home with announcements about Parents Teachers Association Meeting. We hope that this will spark their interest in attending.

We hope to start a 9th grade Parents Teachers Association (in addition to our current PTA) to address the specific concerns of the parents of our incoming freshman class. Would an overlapping group aid these "new" students and their parents in adjusting to the Westinghouse culture? The meetings would be held before the regular PTA meeting so that an extra night out would not be required. We are awaiting the election of a new president of the parents group before we suggest changes.

7

THE STUDENTS ACCEPT
TOTAL QUALITY

"The real definition of education is to learn from
within ourselves. Quality methods provide a
bridge for communication between students.
When communication is good, we can be real
open with those we are working with. Then we
can learn from inside of one another."

Keyur Perikh
A Senior and future doctor currently attending
George Westinghouse Vocational/Technical High School

School is the place where all of society's diseases—crime,
illness, drugs, poverty, violence, child abuse, teenage
pregnancy, and unemployment—converge. Students
unknowingly and unsuspectingly bring these problems into the
school. "The street," television, movies, "Nintendo," friends
who have dropped out or have gotten pregnant, and
openly-discussed sex provides far greater temptations for
young people than ever before. At the same time, there is far
less supervision due to single- or dual-working parents or
separation and divorce.

FACTORS AFFECTING STUDENT LEARNING

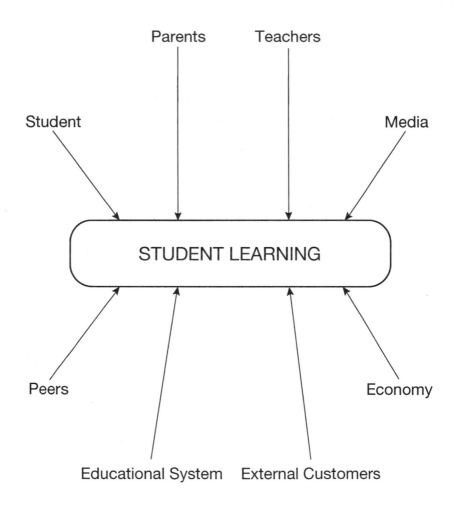

Most public schools have students for 25 hours a week (5 hours a day, 5 days a week). In the best case scenario, schools control 17.5% of their lives. What happens during the other 82.5% impacts on their education. Students lack the sophistication to leave their problems at the school house door. They bring their family, social, and sexual problems into the school because they do not have any other place to turn. One student told me that it was hard for her to concentrate on studying because the sound of gunfire kept disturbing her. (While these problems are more extensive in urban areas, they exist as well in rural and suburban districts.) Frequently, the main adult contact in their life is a teacher. In some cases, it is the only adult contact! Schools help provide some of the stability and structure often missing in young people's lives.

At the same time as schools are addressing these external problems they are expected to produce knowledgeable graduates with a broad range of highly specialized skills. It is difficult for teachers to teach and students to learn foreign languages and computer literacy while coping with problems that the rest of society is either incapable of or unwilling to deal with. It is difficult to teach mathematics to a student if that child has not been fed or if the student has serious problems at home. Many students do not have someone at home to inspire, coach, or help with homework. Since many of our students' parents did not complete high school themselves, they are frequently unable to provide assistance with homework or serve as an educational role model. In addition, children frequently cannot see a direct connection between school and later success in their lives.

Awareness of these conditions cannot deter us from our mission; they can help us to understand better our customers. If we are to succeed, we feel that we have to change the way we deal with teaching and learning. We need to recognize the conditions affecting our students and their families. Using this awareness we must change the way we teach and, within the areas that we control, what we teach.

The greatest challenge in applying Total Quality Education in the schools is applying it in the classrooms with students. Since students are our primary customers, we felt that Total Quality Education would benefit our students if we would develop some means of internally motivating the students. Like most schools, we were still externally motivating our youngsters by having parents and teachers applying external pressures.

Students have always been told that it was important to come to school and to learn. Education works best when *they* see and understand the need to learn. The task indeed seems formidable and we knew that we wouldn't be able to achieve results overnight. The staff felt that we had to demonstrate to the students that we were aware of the difficulties they faced outside school and, at the same time, provide some learning tools to help them master what was taught in the school. If students are to reach their full potential, we have to provide the opportunity. If we expect students to "do the best you can" then we have to provide the means for them to do so.

Research shows that high school students do not do homework, study, or take school seriously. In 1988, a Department of Education survey showed that 17-year-olds spent little time doing homework: 13½% didn't do any homework; almost 21% said homework had not been assigned; almost 28% spent less than 1 hour doing homework; 26% spent between 1 and 2 hours and 12% spent more than 2 hours doing homework. The typical high-school senior does less than an hour of homework an evening.

In order to deal with these situations, educators have been ratcheting down their expectations for students in the hope that students will reach the lowered expectations. Instead, students aim for the floor grade and consider it their ceiling. When they miss, we have failure. With each decrease in expectations, students have failed to meet the lowered standards. Although many teachers believe that most students are capable of doing the work, students frequently appear unwilling to do so. Many students feel that as long as they put in "seat time," they should be passed. We call this a "penitentiary attitude" about school. ("I've served 4 years in this institution, it's time to get out.") Students are used to receiving, from Nintendo and television, immediate gratification and, occasionally, immediate rewards. Telling them to wait 4 years for a high school diploma may be, for some, an unreal expectation.

Not too long ago education was viewed as essential if one was to get ahead in American society. Education must again be seen as a vehicle for social mobility. We need to create an atmosphere of high expectations for students and teachers. We must teach students to see the applicability of what they learn. We should expect students to become self-motivated life-long learners, solve problems, make decisions, work in teams, and think critically. We need to increase the workload for students. Students should no longer compete for grades against their peers. Instead, standards have to be developed and students should be measured against those standards. Having established these criteria we needed a way to help students change what has been accepted in the past.

After we had begun the Staff Recognition and Reward program in 1988, a number of student leaders asked why we were not recognizing and rewarding students who had achieved academically. Most schools recognize and reward athletes. They give athletes jackets, trophies, dinners, and many other visible signs of recognition.

At Westinghouse, and at many other schools, learning frequently takes a back seat to candy sales, pep rallies, school plays, or sports events. While these events are indeed a part of school life, they frequently become the raison d'être of schools. We supply jackets, letters, dinners, and trophies for our athletes but not for our academic achievers. If the business of America is business, then the business of schools is education! We felt that if we were to be successful, we would have to change the culture which acknowledges and admires athletic achievement in the schools but not academic success.

To many students, academic achievement has meant a sign of derision. All kinds of names have been established for those students who succeed in learning. They are called "nerds," "brown-nosers," or worse. Bart Simpson, the television cartoon character, wears a T-shirt which states, "I'm an Underachiever and Proud of it." We decided that Westinghouse would recognize academic achievement. We created a Quality Student Bulletin Board. Every time that report cards are issued the top department academic achievers are listed. We also list the top *schoolwide* academic achievers on the Principal's Quality Student Bulletin Board. A third bulletin board lists students who have

100% Attendance for the term. We were able to convince the Westinghouse Electric Company and National Westminister Bank USA to give Continuous Improvement Scholarships to the three most improved seniors. That is, a student who came into Westinghouse with a low academic average and through hard work and mastery of the material was able to increase significantly his or her grades.

Every term we hold a dinner for the top academic achievers and their parents. We take "Polaroid" pictures and put them into refrigerator magnet frames that read, "You are looking at a Westinghouse Quality Student!" This gift, in recognition of academic accomplishment, is given to the parents. Every time the child or sibling or parent goes to the refrigerator, there is a reminder of academic success.

Every Assistant Principal is sent a list of the top academic achievers in his or her department. The principal has encouraged us to send letters of congratulations to the student's parents and to the feeder school which sent the youngster. This has not only established good will, but it has reinforced the impression that academic excellence is recognized and desired at Westinghouse.

From the outset we were aware that students would have to receive Total Quality training. When we were offered training by National Westminster Bank USA, we requested that students from our Leadership Class receive the same training that the staff received. National Westminster Bank USA generously provided student training at their Manhattan training facility. The students were delighted. By the end of the day of training, they understood the basics of Total Quality. The trip became a yearly highlight.

In 1991, we were able to establish contact with IBM and we expressed an interest in going to their training facility in Palisades, New York. Sherwood "Woody" Bliss who ran the facility and Jim Courage who represents IBM with the New York City Board of Education have been able to provide us the facility for Total Quality training for a weekend. Forty-six people including 23 students, 6 parents, and staff went for a weekend of quality training. We were taught the IBM Quality approach called "Customer Driven Quality." The staff, parents, and students were able to interact in classes and on the basketball courts. Students saw teachers out of the classroom milieu; they saw teachers as human. One parent called to thank me for their child's experience saying, "This was the first time my child has ever been in a hotel. Not only did they have their own bathroom, but their own television and computer as well." The IBM hotel staff could not get over the fact that some students cleaned their rooms before checking out. IBM generously provided another weekend in 1992. Using the P-D-C-A Cycle and questionnaires, they made the training more Westinghouse customer driven. The IBM trainers were able to redirect their normal training techniques, used for their industrial customers, and make them applicable to the Westinghouse High School experience.

We faced several challenges in bringing the Total Quality concepts into the classroom. Limitations on time and funding meant that we could "train" only a limited number of students. Our school year was so curriculum-driven, the best time to do training of students was during the summer. We needed funding for our training program.

We found that the Board of Education had, for a number of years, run a program called *Project Welcome* for incoming 9th graders. In 1991, we randomly selected 200 (out of 400) of our entering 9th grade class to participate in our project. We felt that we would use this group as a control group and would be able to measure the success or failure of the project. We submitted a request to participate in the Board program in order to get funding. The Board of Education wanted us to only use 50 students in the pilot project. We asked that the entire entering class of 400 be allowed to attend. We wanted the Academy to run for 5 days; the Board wanted it to run 3 days. After some negotiation with them, we were funded for 200 students for 3 days. We decided to call project the "Westinghouse Quality Summer Academy." The program was to run shortly before school opened in early September.

IBM had created a cadre of people trained in Total Quality techniques. We decided to use the staff and students who had been trained by IBM to bring Total Quality Education into the classroom. The students would serve as mentors and provide feedback about what changes our customers wanted in our program.

We wanted the Quality Academy to be more than just a tour of our building and the Westinghouse neighborhood. The students were entering Westinghouse frequently lacking skills and values, and we knew that this would cause school failure and difficulties in the world outside. We could not expect students to succeed unless we provided them with the tools and techniques that they needed. Our surveys with staff, parents and students showed that students did know how to study, or listen, or have test-taking skills or know how to make decisions. During the Spring of 1992, the principal and I developed a curriculum, with lesson plans, to teach students to develop these skills. The curriculum was a mixture of school skills and values' clarification. Some of the topics developed, and some questions to be raised in teaching the lessons:

- ◆ Coping with School
  - What are the causes of school failure?
  - How much of a role do others play in causing dropouts?
  - What are the negatives of dropping out?

- ◆ Studying for a Test
  - What resources do I use?
  - Where do I study?
  - When do I study?
  - How do I study?
  - What are some distractions?
  - How do I eliminate distractions?
  - Is there a different way of studying for objective and subjective tests?
  - How do I budget my time?

- ◆ Dealing with Problems which Affect School
  - How can outside events affect school?
  - What steps can I take to cut down on the outside influences impact on school?
  - What do I do when I cannot cut down on outside influences?

- ◆ What do I Want Out of Westinghouse?
  - What do I wish to achieve at Westinghouse?

- What obstacles stand in my way of achieving my goals?
- How do I remove these obstacles?
- Who can assist me at the school?

◆ How Do I Learn Best?
- What are the best methods for learning?
- What are my major distractions?
- How do I eliminate distractions?

◆ Listening and Speaking Skills
- Why should I improve my listening and speaking skills?
- How can I improve my ability to listen?
- How can I improve my ability to speak?

◆ Following Directions
- When do I need to follow directions?
- Why is it important to follow directions?

◆ Time Management
- How can I best manage my time?
- What are some time-wasters?
- How can I eliminate these time wasters?

◆ Setting Priorities
- How do you determine priorities?
- Whose priorities do I choose?
  Mine?
  My parents'?
  Society's?
  School's?
- How do you make up a "to-do" list?

◆ Choosing Friends
- How do I define a friend?
- What qualities should a friend possess?
- When should I break up friendships?

◆ Looking for a Job
- Should I look for work while going to school?
- What is the costs of working while going to school?
- What does a boss look for in hiring people?

- What should I look for in getting a job?
- ◆ Future Goals
  - What will make me happy?
  - How do I select *my* goals?
  - How much influence do I allow others to help me choose my goals?
  - Who should help influence my goals?
  - How do I prioritize my goals?
- ◆ Decisionmaking
  - How do I make choices?
  - What things do I have choices about?
  - What things don't I have choices about?
  - How do I measure my assets and liabilities?
  - Do I know what I want out of life?
  - How do I decide what I want out of life?
- ◆ Choosing a Career
  - What is the difference between a job and a career?
  - What are some of the demands of a career?
  - How do I decide between personal sacrifices and career sacrifices?
- ◆ Self-Image
  - Who am I?
  - What are the components of my identity?
  - What are my attitudes and views of the world?
  - How have my experiences influenced my views?
  - What are my special qualities?
  - What are my values?
  - What are my dreams?
  - What do I want out of life?
- ◆ Critical Thinking
  - What are the techniques of Critical Thinking?
  - How do I develop and use these skills to deal with my life?

We didn't know what to expect with the Quality Academy. Our liaisons at the Board of Education informed us not to expect too much. We were advised that schools which had run a Project Welcome Program in the past hadn't had positive results. Attendance had been low because the Board of Education didn't provide the monies to supply transportation. This meant that students would have to pay for their own transportation for 3 days. We were also asking students to come to school before they were required to. This meant that they would be cutting into their summer vacation. We were told that we should expect a low turnout the first day and that by the final day only a handful of students would be present.

The Assistant Principal–Supervision–English, who was in charge of the Quality Academy, used a "cause and effect diagram" to identify the causes that might lead to the failure of the program. He took steps to eliminate the causes before we ran the program. An action plan was developed assigning jobs and responsibilities to staff and student mentors working in the Quality Academy. Phone calls were made to every student selected. We sent out post cards to students and parents informing them of why the Quality Academy was important. Parents were again called a week before the Quality Academy to remind them.

Day one arrived and with it 245 students. Some students who hadn't been invited by the school had gotten phone calls from students who had been invited. Those not invited were upset that they hadn't been selected. They decided to come and we expanded the class size to accommodate them. By the third day, attendance had dropped off to 187. We distributed surveys at the end of the third day. The survey and the results are shown beginning on the next page.

A debriefing of the Quality Academy staff and student mentors showed that they were less satisfied than the student attendees and their parents. The teachers found it difficult teaching someone else's lesson plans and they wanted input into the development and teaching of the materials. The student mentors wanted a more active role. They enjoyed serving as "big brothers and sisters" to the incoming freshmen and they enjoyed the responsibility and the increased visibility. Student mentors and teachers had found a voice and wanted a say in what they were doing.

We had planned and envisioned the Summer Quality Academy as a unique summer experience and the results of our survey indicated it was. What we failed to do was to make it an integral part of our 9th grade curriculum. Students perceived it as a separate add-on piece of the school. We have decided to infuse elements of the Academy into our regular 9th grade English and Social Studies curricula.

When we distributed report cards at the end of the second marking period (12 weeks into the term) we measured our 9th graders. One hundred twenty-two of them had passed every class. Sixty-two of them had completed the Quality Academy and 60 had not. Of the 56 students who had failed every class, 13 were in the Academy (23.21%) and 43 were not in the Academy (76.79%). It appears that the Quality Academy had little impact for those students who passed every class, but for those students who needed assistance in how to listen, how to take tests, etc., there may have been an impact.

In the Summer of 1993, the Board of Education again funded a Quality Academy. There were now 300 9th graders in the Quality Academy and the Board of Education supplied subway and bus tokens to enable student participants to come to the Academy transportation cost-free.

Project Welcome Summer Quality Academy (1992)
(Survey developed by Robert Johnson, A.P. English, George Westinghouse High School)

	Strongly Agree	Agree	Strongly Disagree	Disagree
1. As a result of my Project Welcome experience, I will have a smooth first term at Westinghouse.	21.5%	63.2%	2.4%	12.9%
2. The tour of the building helped me to learn the locations of important offices on the first floor as well as the locations of shops and classrooms, and other facilities throughout the school.	43.0%	43.7%	1.3%	12.0%
3. I learned a great deal about specific vocational and technical programs at Westinghouse.	24.7%	56.2%	5.6%	13.5%
4. I learned much about the support programs and other services available to me through the presentation of the guidance counselors.	19.0%	62.7%	2.5%	15.8%
5. I have a better understanding of my responsibilities as a student as a result of receiving and discussing the CONTRACT.	26.4%	57.2%	5.7%	10.7%
6. My Project Welcome classroom teacher has given me helpful information and advice.	55.5%	40.1%	2.5%	1.9%

	Strongly Agree	Agree	Strongly Disagree	Disagree
7. My arrival at the school were handled efficiently by school staff and security officers.	13.9%	81.0%	2.8%	2.3%
8. I know that my experience at Westinghouse will be safe and secure.	14.3%	48.4%	10.6%	26.7%
9. I feel as if I have already become a member of the Westinghouse "family".	14.8%	40.1%	17.3%	27.8%
10. I feel that my overall Project Welcome experience was quite helpful to me.	28.5%	61.5%	5.0%	5.0%
11. I am glad that Westinghouse has accepted me as a student.	52.0%	43.4%	2.3%	2.3%

In addition, we have created a pilot class to teach about Total Quality during the regular school year. Students not only learn Total Quality philosophy and history but the use of the Quality tools as well. The course is being designed to teach students how to observe and how to take and analyze data. We want to teach students to take a more active role in their own learning process. The course is being taught to a core group of students who, we envision, will then teach it to other students.

There is so much that must be done to change the learning environment. If we are to succeed, we must identify the needs of the students and understand their culture. We must actively seek their advice and input into much of what we do. Students possess insights that neither parents nor teachers have. We have been taking surveys about studying and homework. One of these surveys is reprinted on the next page. We are currently reformulating our homework policy to reflect the information obtained from the survey.

We have just started to impact student learning. Traditional schools emphasize passive learning and reactive discipline. The Westinghouse vision is to reduce student failure by eliminating the need for students to take courses over again ("rework") and to encourage the students to become life-long, active learners. The new paradigm must be based on active learning and proactive, preventive discipline. If quality is to work, it must be prevention based. This requires that students be responsible for their own learning. It also requires that Total Quality Education begin in the elementary school. By the time students have reached high school, many of their values affecting education have been carved in stone. While Total Quality in high schools can and does have an impact, the impact will be greater the earlier the student is exposed to it.

Many of our students have little joy in their lives. Some of them have seen friends or family members die violently. One young lady informed me that her mother had consistently failed to celebrate her birthday. The schools must celebrate the successes of their students no matter how small (*e.g.,* celebration of birthdays).

Survey on Studying

You do not have to put your name on this survey if you do not wish to.

Answer honestly.

1. Did you study for this test?   YES   NO
    If you did not study skip to Question # 10.
2. How long did you study? TOTAL TIME
    less than ½ hour   ½ hour   1 hour   2 hours
3. Where did you study for this test?
    At home   In my room   In kitchen   In living room
    Somewhere else   Out of house   In library   In school
    On the way to/away from school
4. Did you watch television, listen to radio/stereo, eat while
    you were studying?   YES   NO
5. What time did you study?
    Morning   Afternoon   Evening
6. Do you work after school?   YES   NO
7. Do you do homework?   YES   NO
8. Did you study your class notes?   YES   NO
9. Did you study your homeworks?   YES   NO
10. What percentage of time did you:
    Study homework _____
    Study class notes _____
11. What mark did you get on this test?

We must demand that students do the best that they can. When students hand in minimally or totally unsatisfactory papers, they should be returned with the following questions, "Is this the best you can do? Is this your best work? Is this quality work?" Recognition and reward should not be exclusionary. For some students, daily attendance is an achievement and should be recognized as such. But students should not pass subjects simply because they attend school. We do a disservice to both our students and to our external customers if we pass students who have failed to master material.

We can help build self-esteem and positive self-image by creating bulletin boards with acceptance letters from colleges, enthusiastic letters from employers of our students and graduates. We have a bulletin board in the school with the caption, "We don't want to brag but. . . ." We are looking into hanging mirrors around the school with slogans such as, "We want you to look your best. You're looking at a Quality student."

Total Quality Education isn't just slogans and feel-good messages. It is a change in the basic aspects of running a school. We have been making changes in how we function. We attempted to eliminate grades (in keeping with Dr. Deming's philosophy). We gave pass/fail grades at the end of our first 6 weeks in October 1992. We received phone calls from many of our parents who objected because we weren't acknowledging mastery at the highest level; therefore, we were rewarding a minimally passing grade the same way that we were recognizing an outstanding grade. Our students are accepted to many colleges and universities which require proof of the mastery of subject material.

We are attempting to change our grading standard to passing grades (65–100) and to eliminate the stigma of failing by eliminating failing grades. If a student "fails" a course, he or she would not receive a grade and would merely have the course listed as "no-credit." Students would be promoted on the basis of how many credits they had passed not on how many years they were in the school. "No credit" grades would not be averaged into school averages or ranking. Our computer systems people have informed us that since all of New York City's high schools are on the same system we aren't able to do this. In addition, the colleges and universities that accept our graduates would now have to create a special "Westinghouse" standard. We are looking into changing our grading system but face the difficulty of having our customers wanting it.

We have started aligning our departments. Traditionally students our 9th grade classes read English or American literature while learning about the peoples of India, Southwest Africa, etc., in their Social Studies class. The English and Social Studies Departments have ordered books to be used in the teaching of 9th and 10th grade students (Prentice Hall

Literature, *World Masterpieces,* Englewood Cliffs, NJ, 1991, and Globe Book's *Tapestry: A Multicultural Anthology,* 1993). While students are learning about third-world economies in their history classes, they will be reading third-world literature in their English classes. We expect that this aligned education will ease student learning and comprehension. At the end of the pilot study, we plan to measure the results.

We are working on a program for suspended students. Students who cause discipline problems are usually suspended from the school for a number of days. While they are out of school, they are missing the instruction and structure that many of them vitally need. This frequently results in their failure in school. We are looking into a structured, in-school suspension program where students would be in a classroom all day with material that their teachers supplied and with a proctor to insure that they would be doing it. The Board of Education has not supplied us with the requested funding.

We are using Total Quality tools to help our students to achieve higher grades on the Scholastic Assessment Test (SAT) which they need for admission to college. We did an Isikawa diagram with them to discover how we could help them. We found that one of the reasons for low test scores was because most of them do not take the Preliminary Scholastic Assessment Test (PSAT) in their junior year. Many of them saw the SAT for the first time on the day that they took it. They weren't test prepared. Taking the PSAT would at least make them aware of what was being tested and how it was tested. Our college adviser made a special effort to get juniors to take the PSAT. He phoned homes, wrote letters to parents, and delivered workshops on the need to take these important examinations. We went from 30 juniors taking the PSAT in 1991 to 76 taking the examination in 1992.

In some classes, students are defining the values of various criteria for grading. Traditionally, teachers determine what will be the value of the various components making up a student's grade (*i.e.,* classwork, testing, homework, attendance). In one math class, the students believed that attendance and punctuality should be worth a greater value that the teacher had suggested. Students have accepted the components and, in some cases, have placed higher demands on themselves and their classmates than the teacher would have. What's more, because of student empowerment, a greater percentage of the classes are achieving the higher academic and attendance standards.

Our Leadership Class learns various leadership styles and techniques. We encourage active student involvement in management of this class. Once a month students, selected by the class meet with the principal, making suggestions and asking for a role in running student life in the school.

In one of the more dramatic cases, a staff member used a series of scatter diagrams to show a correlation of grades and study time (in hours). (*See* Chapter 2.) Another scatter diagram shows the correlation between grades and homework missed. Students could see a direct relationship between the number of homework not done and failing grades. One student asked where he was on the graph. The student was asked how many homeworks he had missed and what the grade he had received on the test and then was told, "This mark over here is you!" The staff member reports that since using the scatter diagrams, the number of homeworks handed in by the students has gone up, as have the grades on tests.

If we believe that one of Total Quality Education's basic principles is customer satisfaction, shouldn't we ask our customer's opinion on the service that they receive? Who could better assess customer satisfaction than our primary customer? A few bold teachers have agreed to serve as "guinea pigs" in using a student-generated report card of teachers. They have found that the students are quite perceptive about the classroom and teacher. In most cases, they accurately pinpointed the weaknesses and strengths of the class that they taught. The Student Evaluation of Teachers form is reprinted on the next page.

There is so much variation in our student customers that it is difficult to predict results from specific techniques. For example, teaching a class might cause students to become bored or enthralled. Every teacher will tell you, that a lesson which works in the morning, might not work in the afternoon or vice versa.

Traditionally, schools have focused their interest on the learning. Since students serve as the primary customer of the school, we must address our concerns about the learner. We must ask ourselves: Will our students be life-long learners and people who are capable of making decisions and solving problems? Will our students be able to function outside our classrooms, on their own, without our help? Until we get answers to these questions, we will never be successful in our journey.

The changes that we have been making haven't been meteoric leaps forward but rather small incremental increases. Each one is being used to build on the one before it. Each improvement lays the foundation for the one which follows. Continuous improvement in based on the importance of these small increases.

Student Evaluation of Teachers

(Designed by Franklin P. Schargel, Robert Johnson, and Jeanne Benecke)

	Strongly Agree	Agree	Strongly Disagree	Disagree
1. The work we did helped improve my reading skills.				
2. The work we did helped improve my writing skills.				
3. The work we did helped improve my listening skills.				
4. The work we did helped improve my speaking skills.				
5. The work we did was well-organized.				
6. The work we did was interesting.				
7. I had opportunities to discuss my thoughts and feelings.				
8. I had opportunities to write my thoughts and feelings.				
9. Homework assignments prepared me for classwork.				
10. Homework assignments helped my understanding of classwork.				
11. The teacher cared about us				
12. The teacher cared about me.				

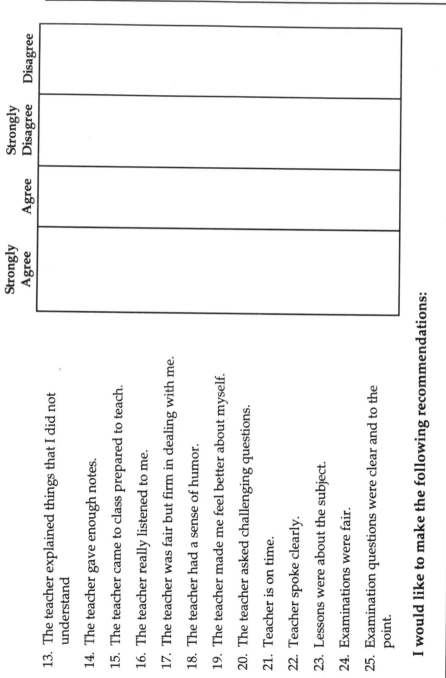

	Strongly Agree	Agree	Strongly Disagree	Disagree
13. The teacher explained things that I did not understand				
14. The teacher gave enough notes.				
15. The teacher came to class prepared to teach.				
16. The teacher really listened to me.				
17. The teacher was fair but firm in dealing with me.				
18. The teacher had a sense of humor.				
19. The teacher made me feel better about myself.				
20. The teacher asked challenging questions.				
21. Teacher is on time.				
22. Teacher spoke clearly.				
23. Lessons were about the subject.				
24. Examinations were fair.				
25. Examination questions were clear and to the point.				

I would like to make the following recommendations:

8

INVOLVING OUR EXTERNAL CUSTOMERS

"Public education in this country is in crisis. America's public schools graduate 700,000 functionally illiterate students every year, and 700,000 more drop out. . . . Public education has put this country at a terrible competitive disadvantage"

David T. Kearns and Denis P. Doyle
Winning the Brain Race: A Bold Plan to Make Our
Schools Competitive (San Francisco: Institute for
Contemporary Studies, 1989:1)

Today's schools please no one—neither parents, children, teachers, politicians, nor businesspeople. Colleges and businesses are having to make do with poorly prepared public school graduates.

Comparisons of our nation's schools with those of foreign countries show our students at the bottom or near the bottom on every assessment. And most scores continue to deteriorate.

In a recent international science achievement survey, our best biology students (in Advanced Placement Classes) received the lowest scores when compared to students of 15 other countries. Overall in science and mathematics, American elementary and high school students performed below students in Canada, China, Japan, Mexico, and Thailand.

Test results are not the only indication. Business leaders have seen the impact of poorly prepared workers on their company's performance and on the American economy. Neither the colleges and universities, who must give remediation courses to high school graduates, nor the business community, which must teach fundamental math to high school and college graduates, are satisfied with America's schools.

If colleges, universities, and businesses have difficulty with the current high school graduate, how will they cope with tomorrow's graduates? Many of today's public school students will be entering colleges and the labor force with poor grades. Some are violent, afflicted with Sexually Transmitted Diseases and AIDS and, occasionally, addicted to drugs. An increasing percentage of America's new workers will be immigrants and minorities or from impoverished families, groups which have tended to have less education and fewer skills than other employees.

Tomorrow's workers will have to generate ideas and have the ability to effectively communicate these ideas to others, both verbally and in writing. This will require workers to possess the ability to develop higher thinking skills and be able to compress complex material and communicate information to others. Mere mathematical computation will not do. Tomorrow workers will have to comprehend and transmit mathematical concepts. Skills such as these are not being taught in most of our nation's schools.

People blame the internal customers of the schools as the source of the problems (i.e., "The students don't care." "Parents aren't involved." "The teachers aren't what they used to be."). Blaming the internal customer for the failure of a business may be unique in education. Envision a hotel manager saying that the hotel was dirty because the occupants came to the hotel without taking a bath or failed to clean up when they left the room.

Today, more businesses are becoming involved with the public schools. In the past, the people in business served as role models on "career days" or as financial backers in projects such as "adopt a school." Involvement was for the short-term, in order to solve an immediate perceived need or for good community relations. Although there is greater involvement by businesses now, the involvement, while generous and well-meaning, is sometimes poorly focussed. In many instances neither the school, the school board, nor the businessperson has determined a realistic and obtainable goal or objective. As David Kearns has written, ". . . [N]o two groups in America know less about each other than business leaders and educators." (David T. Kearns and Denis P. Doyle, *Winning the Brain Race: A Bold Plan to Make Our Schools Competitive*, San Francisco: Institute for Contemporary Studies, 1989:13.)

Much of the help supplied by business has been directed at the post-secondary school level. Such efforts fail to recognize that college students are only as strong as the education they received in the K-12 school system.

The end users of the nation's schools have generally avoided efforts to help public schools systemically change and restructure. "And until schools are reorganized to meet today's challenges, the system will continue to fail." (David T. Kearns and Denis P. Doyle, *Winning the Brain Race: A Bold Plan to Make Our Schools Competitive*, San Francisco: Institute for Contemporary Studies, 1989:7.)

Partnerships need to be formed. External customers must be involved in the schools. They have the most to gain when schools succeed. Businesses and the public schools need to create a symbiotic relationship. "In one sense, business is the customer for the product of our schools, and business should help the education system improve the quality of its output just as it would work with any vendor to upgrade performance." (William H. Kolberg and Foster C. Smith, *Rebuilding America's Workforce: Business Strategies to Close the Competitive Gap*, Homewood, IL: Business One Irwin, 1992:147.)

The long-term interest of the schools and their external customers are the same. There has to be a realization that business will not succeed without their suppliers and the schools will not survive without the external customers. If

American businesses fail, there will not be a tax base to support educational institutions. Conversely, businesspeople must realize that if America's schools fail, there will be a shortage of customers for their products, shareholders for their stocks, workers in their stores and factories and a workforce which will not get its training in the schools. It should be clear that the United States cannot continue to be a global power if it does not improve its schools.

How many businesspeople have seen the new examinations ordered by the state governments? Do these exams meet the minimum standards of the business community? If the business community doesn't know the answer to these essential questions, it is time to find out!

What are current job requirements? Are students being trained in vocational high schools provided with salable skills for today *and tomorrow*? If the school community doesn't know the answer to these essential questions, it is time to find out!

It is the school's responsibility to instill the concepts of quality in its students ("Do the best you can do!" "Do it right the first time!"), but it should be the responsibility of the business community to assist in those efforts. Businesspeople must join the "education team," adding their expertise and knowledge. The answer to the challenges facing America's public schools is not merely to have businesses throw money at the system but help provide the means for the system to change and aid in coalescing the forces interested in saving the system.

Business can assist in the following ways:

◆ **Curriculum**—There is a need to have businesspeople assist in developing, reviewing, and revising curriculum so that graduating students will be trained to take a meaningful role in the marketplace. Colleges and universities can assist high schools to align their curricula with the university curriculum in order to provide a smooth transition to college life.

◆ **Jobs for Students**—Jobs (co-op, after school, summer, and upon graduation) should be created so that students can best see what demands are made upon them in the real-work world. The businessperson can help by assisting the school in training students in quality in the workplace. The student perception of the business community which has come from the media frequently is not true, and oftentimes is unrealistic.

◆ **Paid Externships**—Many teachers lack or have outdated knowledge of the business community. Industry should hire teachers during the summer so that teachers can upgrade their skills. Many trade, technical, and business education teachers need to learn the latest business techniques. Many academic teachers have not been part of the outside workplace; many came into teaching directly from college. Externships are a win-win situation. By bringing teachers into businesses and training them, they will have the latest knowledge and current expertise needed to teach the students. Businesses, therefore, will not have to put a great deal of time and money into training high school graduates.

◆ **Business Training Workshops**—Principals, teachers, and a selected core of students should be invited to attend on-going workshops conducted by businesses to learn their techniques in quality training, interviewing and management.

◆ **Businesspeople on Loan**—Business personnel with skills in teaching quality improvement techniques should be sent to the schools to teach classes for a day, a week, a month, or a semester. In addition, the businessperson might also provide school personnel with practical business advice. They can help students prepare résumés, give "mock interviews," and help retiring teachers prepare for new careers.

◆ **Pressure Group**—Industry should encourage state legislatures, local school boards, and the federal government to increase spending for education and help create the minimum quality standards.

◆ **Funds**—Money is needed in schools to help establish quality incentive awards for teachers and students and to create scholarships for quality students.

Since education and training for college and employment continue to be the primary mission at George Westinghouse Vocational and Technical High School, we have focussed our attention on achieving these goals. As a result of our efforts to involve our external customers in the workings of George Westinghouse, we have achieved the following:

◆ Chase Manhattan Bank agreed to hire one of our students. At the end of the term, we asked how and if the student could have been better prepared. Banking officials informed us that our student didn't speak properly. We were concerned about the possibility of future employment for our students both at Chase Manhattan Bank and other businesses. We asked the Brooklyn Union Gas Company and Chase Manhattan Bank to give our students "mock interviews" and they agreed with the Chase assessment. Our principal hired three speech teachers. Now a student cannot graduate from Westinghouse High School unless he or she has successfully completed 1 year of speech. This year Chase hired 27 of our students. In December 1992, Chase Manhattan Bank gave us a large number of used and broken computers to train our students in the use of computers and computer repair.

◆ Business-School Advisory Councils have been established in the electronics, woodworking, and optical areas. Council members from business, industry and our staff meet regularly with the principal to suggest ways to upgrade our programs and make our students more employable.

◆ Our school has also been visited by numerous business leaders who have donated equipment and supplies. The Motorola Foundation recently donated money to enable us to buy Total Quality Management textbooks to be used in class.

◆ Our Woodworking Council told us that our woodworking program was excellent, but they wouldn't hire any of our students because the students were being trained to work with wood and not with laminates. The Council generously supplied us with a used laminating-cutting machine and scrap laminates to work with. Everybody won! Our students received state-of-the-art training. Our school received machinery that we couldn't afford to buy and the woodworking industry received workers who didn't need additional training.

◆ The International Business Machine Corporation (IBM) provided two weekends of TQ training at their Palisades facility for members of our staff, our student body, and our parents. This has helped facilitate our Total Quality training for our staff. It has helped us to train students and parents in the process.

◆ National Westminster Bank USA and the Westinghouse Electric Corporation have agreed to fund multiple-year continuous improvement scholarships to our most academically-improved graduating students.

◆ Perhaps our greatest success came when officials from a Japanese photocopier company came to visit Westinghouse. They looked at our process, determined it was correct, and agreed to help our students. We have formed a partnership with them. Our students, are being paid to repair their photocopiers and fax machines.

Westinghouse High School is providing strong academic preparation for students. This will prove essential if graduates wish to qualify for demanding jobs. By building networks with our external customers we are developing School-to-Work opportunities for our graduates who prefer not to go to college immediately.

Westinghouse is fortunate to be in close proximity to three institutions of higher learning. We have been meeting with them in order to discuss joint concerns.

When we asked officials at Polytechnic University how we could gain admission for our graduates, they said that their Scholastic Assessment Test scores were too low. We informed them that many of our students are living in poverty. Our students couldn't avail themselves of Scholastic Assessment Test review classes. Polytechnic University offered to have some of their students tutor our students for the Scholastic Assessment Tests. As a result, we had 27 students regularly taking the Scholastic Assessment Test course offered by Polytechnic Institute. One of our students earned 1,100 points on the January 1993 examination.

In addition, Polytech has created advanced courses in mathematics and science for our students to take at the University and they are providing library privileges for some students. Polytechnic is furnishing college students to work in our College Office. They are supporting visits from the college's National Society of Black Engineers and Society of Women Engineers. We are one of only two high schools in New York State to have a chartered Junior National Society of Black Engineers. Thirty-two students were members in the 1992–93 school year. Twenty more students joined at the 1993–94 school year. NSBE members participated in science and technology competitions and advanced engineering workshops. In 1993, Polytech created four $8,000-per-year scholarships just for Westinghouse students.

TQ provides a common language between schools and businesses. The university and business communities have been active supporters of what we have been doing because they know of the benefits of Total Quality Management.

On October, 1, 1991, the Chief Executive Officer of Ricoh, Inc., the Japanese photocopier and camera company, spoke at Quality Forum VII. He cited the story of Ricoh's recall of defective photocopy machines at a cost of $59,000; his audience was duly impressed. Had the defect been caught at the design stage the cost would have been $35. The audience, composed of quality experts, understood the need to catch defects at the earliest stages of production. Yet, in America, there is clearly a lack of understanding by our industrial leaders of the need to teach Total Quality Management in our nation's schools. Maybe the businesspeople can understand the words of Lester Thurow, in *Head to Head*, that "In the 21st century, the education and skills of the work force [will] end up being the dominant competitive weapon."

America's workers must not only possess technological skills but also the desire to continue learning, on their own, so they can adjust to the rapid changes taking place in the workplace and in the real world. Today's worker has the opportunity to work with fiber optics, photocopiers, facsimile machines, cellular phones, and computers. These products didn't exist 20 years ago.

The success of the Japanese is not based solely on their use of Total Quality Management, but also on their realization of the importance of the worker. This factor is sadly lacking in most of America's TQM efforts. Some business leaders believe that workers are expendable. Some feel that immigration and technology will overcome the gap that American schools are failing to fill. We are an endangered species if we believe that technology is the answer to our nation's needs.

9

SHORT-TERM RESULTS

We were visited by a professor from a well known Ivy League School of Education who entered our school with the words, "We at _____ University do not believe that you are doing what you say you are doing." He proclaimed that he would spend a day checking our statistics, speaking to staff, students, external customers, and parents. At the end of the day he stated, "We were wrong! You are doing what you say you are doing. I just don't see any dramatic change."

Americans have come to expect instant results. We have instant coffee, instant breakfast, and instant pudding. Joan Rivers says she has a friend who stands in front of the microwave yelling, "Hurry! Hurry!" Americans are impatient and frustrated if results do not come as quickly as we would like.

As gardeners know, if you wish to remove something that you do not wish in the garden, you must remove it from the roots. If you remove only those portions above the ground, the weed will return. Total Quality Education removes the root causes instead of dealing with the symptoms. This makes the Total Quality process slow. We compare it to moving a glacier.

At the time of the writing of this book, we have been immersed in the process for 3 years. We are still learning. What follows are our short-term results.

INTERNAL CHANGES

Perhaps the greatest change has taken place with our faculty. They have come to accept, in some cases slowly, that change is taking place in our school. The staff now sits on committees, and have agreed to advise school clubs, attend brainstorming workshops, and meet with businesspeople. They are not paid to do this. Perhaps they do this because they see that the Total Quality process works. They are making suggestions and recommendations for changing our process. There is still staff skepticism and criticism. The younger staff has accepted the process more readily than our senior staff. Almost every faculty meeting addresses one issue in our quality efforts. Subject-area department meetings frequently discuss the quality improvement of instruction. We have begun a newsletter, *Total Quality,* to describe the changes taking place. Teacher union grievances against the principal have gone from 26 (1991) to 0 (1992).

Through the "New York Working" Grant we have established a Job and Career Placement Office, which functions 12 months of the year. This office provides job placement for students while they are attending school and during the summer. It provides career training and placement for those graduates who are going directly to the world of work.

We are holding interdepartmental meetings. "Turf" battles have diminished as vocational and academic teachers meet to discuss student behavior in their classrooms.

DONATED EQUIPMENT AND SUPPLIES

The school has raised more than $1 million for new or additional programs and services. We are one of six charter New York City high schools (and the only vocational school) to receive $143,000 a year for 3 years to establish a year-round on-site employment office.

BUSINESS ASSISTANCE

Business-School Advisory Councils in electronic, woodworking, and optics suggest ways to upgrade our programs and improve student employability.

WITH OUR PARENTS

Our Parents Teachers Association has grown from 12 members (1991) to 211 (1992). At the same time the parents raised the cost of dues from $3 a year to $10 a year. Attendance at meetings is still influenced by outside forces such as the weather and our ability to do mailings and make phone calls. Family Night has become institutionalized and takes place every year. Some parents have participated in our Steering Committee meetings. For the first time in memory, parents now compete for PTA offices.

WITH OUR STUDENTS

Our efforts with the students have just begun. We want students to internalize the need for education. In September 1993, we began to teach an interdisciplinary Total Quality class to the students who attended the IBM Quality weekend. The class mixes the history of the Total Quality movement with the philosophy of Deming, Juran, etc. The students are learning how to work on teams and are assisting one another with classwork. In addition, the course uses mathematics, statistics, and the quality tools. Students use the tools to address the challenges of learning in the school. The primary teacher of the course is the Quality Coordinator. He is assisted by the Statistical Quality Coordinator. The Statistical Quality Coordinator teaches students how to use the tools of Total Quality Management in the educational setting. Guest lecturers are called upon, both from inside the school and from the surrounding college community and local businesses, to assist in teaching the student's research and writing techniques. By taking this course, students will be more valuable in the workplace and in universities teaching Total Quality Management.

We plan that these students will serve to "turnkey" other students. They will become mentors and instructors in the

Spring 1994 term. Staff members with "free periods" are encouraged to participate in the class with the students.

Our dropout rate, as reported by the Board of Education, was 7.8% (1990–91), falling to 5.3% (1991–92), and falling again to 2.1% in 1992–93. New York City's dropout rate was 17.2% during the same time period.

Students have become more involved in the school. They provide peer tutoring and escort senior citizens on shopping tours. School extracurricular activities have grown. We have added the following clubs: Darts, Chess, Computers, Leadership, Math, Optical, Asian, Hatian-Creole, and African-American Culture.

We were concerned that many of our students weren't properly preparing themselves for entry into college. We decided (in 1992) to focus our attention on our junior students. Through the use of several of the quality tools we were able to increase the number of junior students taking the Preliminary Scholastic Assessment Examination (PSAT) from 30 to 76. That is an increase of 153%. We have just begun two Scholastic Assessment Classes, one in English and one in Mathematics, in order to increase our student's capabilities in taking this important college entrance examination. Fifty-five of our students are taking a weekly SAT preparatory class at Polytechnic University.

Seventy-two percent of our graduates are going to college. Slightly less than one-half of them are the first in their family to finish high school.

Our students are currently receiving scholarships for continuous improvement. These scholarships are multiple-year commitments from our industrial partners, National Westminster Bank USA and the Westinghouse Electric Corporation.

Requests for admission to Westinghouse have grown. We now receive about 10 applications for every seat.

COLLEGE COLLABORATIVES

Pratt Institute, Polytechnic University, and New York City Technical College have agreed to run coordinated programs with Westinghouse High School. Project Care allows our students to take courses at the colleges while they are still attending Westinghouse.

In order to create a seamless transition from the school to the workplace, we have created with New York Technical College a 2+2 Tech-Prep program. Students at Westinghouse take courses at New York City Technical College at the same time they are completing their high school career at Westinghouse. We infuse additional academic courses in the form of "Tech-Prep Mathematics" and "Tech-Prep English" to boost the potential for success at college. At the college students are engaged in taking advanced vocational programs that Westinghouse alone could not provide.

As a result of positive experiences with the college, they have provided additional services to both staff and students. Our top-level college-bound students use the biology, chemistry, and physics laboratories at New York City Tech. Twenty-two faculty members took free courses at the college. Over 100 Westinghouse students have received college credits for completing courses taken at the college. City Tech faculty have provided college and employment seminars for our students.

INCREASED RECOGNITION

We were honored to have been selected by the American Society for Quality Control (ASQC) and the American Association for School Administrators (AASA) to be part of their video, *Continuous Quality Improvement: A New Look For Education.* Claire Crawford-Mason is in the process of finishing a 30 minute video on the changes we are making, *Quality in Education: Deming in the Classroom.*

Dr. Peggy Siegel and Ms. Sandra Byrne of the National Alliance for Business visited 11 sites during 1992. The sites included 4 industrial winners of the Malcolm Baldridge Award and 6 school districts and one school. We were privileged to have been selected as one of the sites visited. The report, *The Cutting Edge of Common Sense, Using Total Quality to Reinvent Education*, looks for common features in the schools and businesses visited. Quoting from this journal, "The camaraderie among administrators, teachers, and students at this Brooklyn-based high school thrives in sharp contrast to the metal detector and security guards stationed at the front door." (p. 17.)

We have been asking ourselves several questions which we are, at this time, unable to answer:

- ◆ Will our short-term results hold up over time?
- ◆ Can we credit the process for our successes?
- ◆ Should we blame the process for some failures? Is the process at fault or our lack of understanding at how to apply it correctly?
- ◆ Have we created an environment which is not "individual dependent"? That is, if the Quality Coordinator or principal leave, will the process continue? For some of the industrial models we have been benchmarking, when the Chief Executive Officer left, the process ceased to function.

On June 18, 1993, we recieved the following letter:

"Dear Mr. Rappaport:

I am very pleased to hear of the positive strides taken by George Westinghouse Vocational and Technical High School toward improving the educational environment at the school.

I commend you and the entire Westinghouse community for instituting a Total Quality Education Initiative that has increased parent and teacher involvement, and most importantly, improved student outcome. I am thrilled that Westinghouse's Initiative has encouraged so many new parents to participate in the school, that the student dropout rate is down, and that the graduation rate is up. It is truly an encouraging sign that so many of your students are now opting to further their education by going on to college. Please also extend my thanks to the many corporate partners who have joined your school in this important effort.

On behalf of eight million New Yorkers, I applaud the efforts of the George Westinghouse High School to provide a quality education for all its students.

Sincerely,

David N. Dinkins
MAYOR

More important than the accolades are the positive responses we have been receiving from our customers. It is their acknowledgment and encouragement which makes the effort worthwhile and leads us to believe we are on the right road.

10

WHAT'S NEXT AT WESTINGHOUSE?

Total Quality Education has the ability to produce greater efficiency by eliminating student failure, empowering staff, involving parents, and connecting external customers to the school.

At Westinghouse, we know we've just begun the process and know that we are on the right track. Changes are constantly taking place. Our internal and external customers are satisfied with our achievements to date, but we cannot become complacent and settle for short-term success. Westinghouse is a much better school now than it was 3 years ago, but not as good as it will be tomorrow. School transformation is a long-term process that requires careful planning and implementation. Continuous improvement continues to be our operational byword.

Our plan is to continue the process, adding new components within the fiscal restraints imposed by the State and the City of New York. (According to the President of the

New York City Board of Education, the past 4 years has seen a cut of $1.4 billion in the New York City educational budget. The 1993–94 New York City High School budget was reduced by 12.75% or $30 million.) Many of the changes discussed below do not require the infusion of funds, and therefore should be easy to implement.

ADMINISTRATION

Monthly the principal meets with the administrative and supervisory staff. At these cabinet meetings, the principal has placed the issue of Quality on the agenda. Basically he asks, "How are we going to better deliver services to our customers?" Each assistant principal discusses one area under his or her control ("How are we reducing failure?").

Each supervisor meets with their department monthly and focuses on quality improvement. The role of supervision in the school is shifting. Supervisors are creating ongoing instructional teams to plan, manage, and improve their own work without traditional supervision. These self-directed teams are evolving curriculum, testing techniques, and learning how to use the tools in the classroom. Department supervisors are asking teachers to discuss which management obstacles are preventing them from doing their jobs well. We are beginning to remove those hurdles. Department meetings now have classroom teachers sharing teaching experiences and techniques. This is in lieu of the traditional department meetings of top-down management emphasizing administrative messages.

Joint department meetings are planned between academic and technical subjects. These joint meetings help break down the walls which exist between academicians and vocational teachers.

We are beginning to change the way we do classroom observations. Traditionally, observations are done by the supervisor. Now several teachers have started observing each other and are making suggestions about how to improve instruction.

ALUMNI

We are making efforts to revive a sadly flagging Alumni Association. Many of our graduates have the ability to serve as mentors and role models for our present students. Some have contacts at our nation's universities and businesses and can aid in college and career placement. Some work at firms which are practicing Total Quality Management and can provide training for faculty and students. Our alumni can also serve as volunteer tutors to our at-risk students.

EXTERNAL CUSTOMERS

We are also focussing on our external customers. We have begun discussions with one of our corporate sponsors to initiate a Corporate and College Quality Council which will provide periodic Total Quality training and advice to the school. We are making an effort to involve local small businesses in the school. We can provide meeting space and trained professionals who can teach their workers Total Quality Management techniques, computer skills, and an array of other customer-driven skills. They can meet our students, provide mock interviews, and real jobs.

We have to reach out to our suppliers—all of the feeder schools which send us students. We can begin preparation of their students while they are in the middle school. Our students can help prepare their students for entry into high school. They can serve as tutors, mentors, or a "third ear."

Our outreach to the college community will continue. Discussions are now taking place regarding the development of a joint-grant writing effort.

PARENTS

We felt that we had created an effective outreach to parents and thought that we had caused parents to internalize the Total Quality process. However, membership in the Parents Teachers Association started to slide. We had become overly optimistic and complacent. We have developed knowledge from our mistakes and we are profiting from our missed steps. Now we realize that we cannot take any component for granted. The

P-D-C-A-cycle must be used repeatedly to renew and refresh the process. We plan to retrace the steps that we originated with our parents. We have asked their assistance in formulating a new parent survey.

We must provide Total Quality training for our parents. Some of our parents work for companies that practice Total Quality and we plan to use them as facilitators to turnkey other parents in the techniques and tools of Total Quality. We need to demonstrate how the tools can assist them in removing root cause challenges to the issues which face them. We have the ability to help them create Action Plans and Cause and Effect diagrams to increase parent turnout at Parents Teachers meetings.

Our surveys have shown that parents wish to help their children succeed. However, it is difficult for parents to aid in their children's education if the parents do not possess the skills and training in reading, mathematics, and technology that the school is capable of providing. Many parents would like to complete their high school education and raise their own literacy. Some parents have expressed an interest in learning how to use a computer. Our foreign-language-speaking parents would like to learn to speak English. We have requested permission from the Board of Education to open the building to our parents. Due to a lack of available funding, we have been denied permission. We will continue to pursue this venture. We feel it is important to us, our parents, and society at-large.

We are making an effort to have the parents treat education more seriously. We are now asking parents not to make medical appointments for their children during school hours and not to take the student on vacation when school is in session. We are requesting that parents have their children read to them and to provide space in their homes to encourage studying and the completion of homework.

JUST IN TIME TRAINING

One of the reasons for Japanese industrial success is their ability to focus on "just in time" manufacturing. This means, that they produce products when they need them. In America, we produce manufactured goods in advance, sometimes, far in advance. Americans produce "just in case" it sells. The Japanese save money by not warehousing.

In American education, we educate students "just in case" they may use the material. Schools must be given enough latitude to develop curricula with parents, students, and external customers to suit the needs of their customers. In this era of mandated, politically-inspired curriculum, we must allow those closest to the problem develop the solution. Material taught in classes has to be examined for its applicability and relevance to the world of today and tomorrow.

Our greatest efforts must be directed at our staff and our students, for no one else plays a greater role in changing the instructional process.

STAFF

We need to actively seek increased staff participation. Quality is not just the teachers' job; everyone must be drawn into the paradigm shift. Secretaries, school aides, security officers, and cafeteria workers need to join the rest of the school in this venture. Each person must ask himself or herself, "How do *I* improve the quality at Westinghouse?"

Cross-functional learning teams are being established. These teams, composed of faculty members in both the academic and technical areas, will work in concert to make the best decisions for the school as a whole. Departmental concerns are put aside for the good of the school.

The challenges are many. The greatest challenge is to classroom teachers. The teachers are the facilitators of learning, not the managers of learning. New techniques are being developed to make learning more interactive and less teacher dominated. When the teacher asks questions, it should be done in a manner that encourages critical thinking skills and not merely be a regurgitation of facts. Teachers are starting to ask, "How do I interest this student?"

Students are helping define Quality in the classrooms. In vocational classes, teachers are exhibiting each student's work and asking other students to give the work a grade. Students are then asked how the grade was obtained. A consensus is formed so that students can distinguish merely passing work from "masterpiece" quality. We are expanding this experiment into academic classes. In Social Studies classes homework papers and tests rated "excellent" are on display so that students have an established benchmark. In a few classes, student work is returned with the comment, "Is this your best work?" "Is this quality work?" Frequent discussions take place regarding grading.

We are continuing our efforts to eliminate nonpassing grades. Students who do not master the instructional material, will be given a "no credit" for the class on their report cards. We will base promotion and graduation on performance and mastery of the material—not on years spent at the school. "No credit" course grades will not appear on the students' transcripts.

In some departments, teams of teachers are joining together to create examinations which test critical thinking and problem solving skills instead of rote memorization. We are using cooperative learning techniques in order to foster team skills. Slower learning students are being assisted by more advanced students in class teams. This team effort helps all students. The mentor student has an improved self-image and reinforces his own learning while aiding his classmate. The mentored student has a friend giving assistance and learns more easily. We are experimenting with team-testing in which students help one another with answers to thought-provoking test questions.

Several members of our teaching staff have been bringing the process into the classroom. One teacher asks her students what components should be used in determining grades and what proportion of their grade should be based on homework, on attendance, on tests, and on classwork. She has been using scatter diagrams to show a correlation between doing homework and grades on class tests. Scatter diagrams are also being used to show a correlation between grades on tests and study time. Students can visually see the relationship. As a result, they are spending more time doing homework and studying and are achieving a greater mastery with the material. Another teacher has divided his Carpentry Shop into five corporations. Each corporation has established a Board of Directors including a Chief Executive Officer, Chief Financial

Officer, and an Advertising Executive. The class is developing products which each corporation will sell. A third teacher has made his Social Studies classroom more interactive by having students develop questions to be used on their examinations. Two other teachers, one from the Social Studies Department and one from the English Department, are using cooperative learning as a technique to get students more actively involved in their own learning. We are developing surveys to measure the degree of satisfaction students and parents are receiving from these experiments. We plan to access the success of these ventures through the collection of data regarding mastery of the material learned.

Our Steering Committee has found it difficult to address some of the issues because of increased membership. Smaller, more manageable task forces have been developed to deal with newly created issues. We have formed Incentives, 75th Anniversary, Discipline, and Cafeteria Task Forces. These task forces are gathering material and will report back to the Steering Committee and the Principal. The Steering Committee has been empowered: It has the knowledge and tools necessary to assess issues and the freedom to implement actions without fear.

Not every member of our Steering Committee can attend every meeting. Some are taking courses at college. Some staff members must provide child care for their own children. Some students must arrange to be home for younger children arriving home from school. Students and staff frequently have second jobs after school. We need to develop a mechanism which will create a consistant core of attendees to our Steering Committee.

STUDENTS

Education was once seen as a vehicle for upward social mobility. Students appreciated the value of an education. We must make extensive use of successful graduates, college students, and members of the business community to teach the value of succeeding in school. Academic success and achievement must be recognized and rewarded. Parents should receive positive phone calls when their children do well. This takes time and money. We are creating bulletin boards, captioned "We are proud of our successful students," with students' acceptance letters from colleges, employers, and the military.

Looking into most classrooms you will find the teacher doing the work. The teacher is lecturing and the student is minimally involved. This may be one of the reasons why students are apathetic and bored. The classroom with the greatest student participation is the kindergarten. Maybe that is why the students seem so happy and involved. As students' progress from grade to grade, their participation in class diminishes. When ultimately they reach college, the teacher does all of the work and the student merely listens. Teachers lecture, pouring information into supposedly empty vessels. Compare the excitement in a kindergarten student's face and the dull look in the eyes of a high school student. We blame the curriculum. It is the process that is at fault.

Many educators believe that they are the workers—the "givers" of learning. Others serve as "pied pipers"—leading students to education. We at Westinghouse are devising and testing techniques in which students want to learn, on their own, for their entire life. By the teacher being "the worker" the burden of education falls on the teacher and not the student. This causes the continual need for extrinsic motivation and not intrinsic learning. It is the student who should be the worker in education. Students at Westinghouse are being trained to be responsible for their own learning. At Westinghouse High School, we believe that teachers should merely provide the tools and direction while the students do the work. Teachers should simply guide the educational process.

We must build a bridge from external motivation (from teachers and parents) to internal motivation. But the change must be incremental. Students must come to feel that they have a say in what they are doing. We are planning to have greater student involvement in developing curriculum, school calendars, and school events.

Taking of the joy out of learning took a number of years; putting it back will take at least as long. When the change ultimately clicks in, it will not like a light switch—from off to on. It will be achieved like a dimmer switch gradually bringing light into a room.

Schools have spent little time teaching students how to learn. The Total Quality Management class is designed to teach students how to observe, gather, and analyze data. We are doing this so that they can take a more active role in their own learning process.

At Westinghouse, we are forming student "reading teams" which will encourage students to read in groups. This method has worked in industry and it fosters comprehension, discussion, and a love for the written word. These groups will meet during lunch periods and/or after school. Reading groups will be small, voluntary, self-directed, and not established by the school administration. The selection of the books will come from the team members and determined by general agreement. Books should be easily and quickly read. The school administration will provide the meeting room and a sufficient number of books.

Perhaps our vision was best expressed in a *New York Times* editorial on October 28, 1991: "No issue is more important to New York City's future than the performance of its public schools. The economy cannot prosper without a well-educated labor force; the city's huge immigrant population cannot be assimilated without good schools. . . . But the city's schools are not plummeting toward catastrophe. Indeed, by some performance measures, they have at least held their own and may actually have improved over the last 20 years. What has changed most dramatically is the demand imposed by society. The schools must now educate a population that is markedly poorer, more socially handicapped, and less competent in English than 20 years ago. And they must prepare students for jobs that require far more skills than ever before. The schools have to run a lot faster just to keep pace with the new demands."

We are attempting to follow the philosophy of Frank Caplan, President of Quality Services, Inc., who stated at a NEQI Conference in July, 1989: "Basically what is needed is to incorporate portions of the subject matter of the Quality Sciences into every course taken by anyone in the United States from kindergarten through graduate school. Our entire society needs to become thoroughly at ease in the area of Quality, in all its implications, to be able to compete in the future."

Westinghouse is attempting to integrate the goals of our Quality improvement process into our day-to-day and long-range plans and activities. We remind ourselves continually that the process is not a separate function or add-on to our normal jobs. It has to become so ingrained into our daily existence that using the process is automatic. Continuous Quality will help us better meet the requirements of each of our internal and external customers.

11

THE FUTURE OF TOTAL QUALITY MANAGEMENT IN EDUCATION

The winds of change are blowing through the halls of education. Change is inevitable. It is not a question of *if* the change will take place, but more a question of *when and what* will happen. The planned unification of Europe, the disintegration of Communism, and the end of the Cold War era will change things even faster. Multi-national companies will seek out the lowest cost laborers to produce products and will find the best technologically prepared workers to design machinery and computers. If America's frontline educators fail to transform education, the graduates of our schools will be left out of the workplace shift. If we, the educators, fail to make the necessary changes, they will be imposed on us by others.

Spurred by the realities of a loss of market share caused in the global marketplace and an increasingly critical American buying public, American business community and government officials are recommending that schools use Total Quality Management as the vehicle to restructure and reorganize the schools. Firms like AT&T, Colgate-Palmolive, Corning, IBM, 3M Corporation, Motorola, and Xerox have generously made their training workshops and personnel available to the school. As Total Quality Management practitioners, they believe that Total Quality Education will work to transform the school system.

People in business and the government realize that if we don't deal with the educational problems now, we're going to deal with them in the generations to come. They understand that if American industry is to re-enter the marketplace as "world class," it must focus on American education. We, as a nation, can no longer afford simplistic responses to complex problems. Total Quality Management empowers schools, just as it empowered businesses, to focus attention on the challenges presented to education. Just as the "quality revolution" of American business began in the 1980's, education will be the cornerstone of quality in the 1990's and beyond.

Part of the concern of the policymakers deals with the cost of education. Spending on education has risen rapidly in the past 20 years, but educational skills have not. If we could improve the educational level in New York State by 5%, we would improve education for 1,320,250 students and reduce the cost of education up to $1.01 billion. Imagine if we could improve the educational level in New York State by 10%. We would improve education for 2,645,000 students and reduce the cost of education up to $2.02 billion. Bob Galvin, former chairman of Motorola, believes that our GNP could rise by ½–1% per year if we instituted a national policy on quality. We are faced with an alternative. Either fix the educational system now or pay the cost of our failure to do it later.

Ten years ago, *A Nation At Risk: The Imperative for Education Reform* (The National Commission on Excellence in Education, commissioned by Secretary of Education T.H. Bell; April 1983:4), a national study, gave an urgent call to reform our nation's schools:

> "Our Nation is at risk. Our once unchallenged pre-eminence in commerce, industry, science, and technological innovation is being overtaken by

competitors throughout the world. . . . The educational foundations of our society are presently being eroded by a rising tide of mediocrity that threatens our very future as a Nation and a people. What was unimaginable a generation ago has begun to occur—others are matching and surpassing our educational attainments.

If an unfriendly foreign power had attempted to impose on America the mediocre educational performance that exists today, we might well have viewed it as an act of war. . . . We have even squandered the gains in student achievement made in the wake of the Sputnik challenge. Moreover, we have dismantled essential support systems which helped make those gains possible. We have, in effect, been committing an act of unthinking, unilateral educational disarmament.

Our society and its educational institutions seem to have lost sight of the basic purposes of schooling, and of the high expectations and disciplined effort needed to attain them."

Yet the report did not produce a change in the organization or results of the schools.

Test scores have continued to stagnate. *Adult Literacy in America,* a 1993 report financed by the United States Department of Education, states (as reported in *Newsday,* September 9, 1993:5) that reading levels among young adults have declined since the 1980's. "Young adults scored 11 to 14 points lower than those of the same age surveyed eight years ago." Madeline M. Kunin, Deputy Secretary of Education, stated (as reported in the *New York Times,* September 9, 1993:A22), "The overall education level of Americans has increased in terms of schooling and even in fundamental literacy. But the demands of the workplace simultaneously have vastly increased. We simply are not keeping pace with the kinds of skills required in today's economy."

It is obvious that today's schools are not meeting the challenge of educating our young people. Dissatisfaction with the schools is similar to dissatisfaction with businesses. Educators need to learn that, just as business customers leave companies because of poor service, students and parents leave schools because of poor achievement.

There have been numerous government studies recommending change and the establishment of educational goals. The most comprehensive were the goals proposed in 1989 by the National Governors Association. These goals were later endorsed by President Bush and the Congress. This plan proposed to improve our country's educational system by the year 2000 by providing direction and guideposts. These goals require systemic restructuring of schools, not merely extending school days or lengthening the school year. By establishing these goals, the Federal and state governments focussed America's attention on its schools and the need to improve the educational process.

The Six National Education Goals

1. All children in America will start school ready to learn.
2. The high school graduation rate will increase to at least 90 percent.
3. American students will leave grades' four, eight, and twelve having demonstrated competency in challenging subject matter, including English, mathematics, science, history, and geography; and every school in America will ensure that all students learn to use their minds well, so they may be prepared for responsible citizenship, further learning, and productive employment in our modern economy.
4. U.S. students will be the first in the world in science and mathematics achievement.
5. Every adult American will be literate and will possess the knowledge and skills necessary to compete in a global economy and exercise the rights and responsibilities of citizenship.

6. Every school in America will be free of drugs and violence and will offer a disciplined environment conducive to learning.

President Clinton, in his former role as the head of the National Governors' Association, has affirmed these goals. But setting goals and achieving them are two different things.

President Bush proposed "America 2000—Excellence in Education" as a method of achieving the objectives suggested by the National Education Goals. By calling his plan America 2000 rather than Education 2000, he envisioned the challenge as one facing this country, instead of one merely facing education. By outlining goals, he established a mission for education in this country. Included in the President's 10-part proposal was:

◆ The creation of 535 nontraditional "New American Schools" which would be provided with seed money for the best teachers, new learning methods and advanced technology.

◆ Establishment of "Merit Schools" to reward schools that make notable progress toward the achievement of the National Education Goals.

◆ Provide teacher training programs in each state.

◆ Aid states in developing and implementing flexible teacher certification programs.

◆ Encourage and test different methods for "educational choice," including providing parents with a voucher for private schools, if they so choose.

◆ Permit states to use voluntary National Assessment tests in English, science, math, history, and geography in grades 4, 8, and 12.

America 2000 fell short when it suggested that the voucher system would solve the causes of educational failure. The establishment of 535 New American Schools—one in each Congressional and Senatorial District shows how politics plays a role in the educational system. By focussing on the mission without identifying the method or providing the means to achieve it, simply identified the program as rhetoric. President Bush's proposal was ultimately rejected by both the House of Representatives and the Senate.

The Federal government contributes about 6% of the total national educational funding. The major cost is borne by the states. Hardpressed because of current economic conditions, states have been cutting educational expenses, not increasing them. The focus has become one of improving the schools with less money being spent.

More and more governors have come to believe that Total Quality Education will help to achieve more with less money. Several have formed groups and have held conferences looking into existing educational models. Texas Governor Ann Richards' *Critical Linkages*, Colorado Governor Roy Romer's National Quality and Education Conference: *Quality & Education: Strategies for Transformation*, and Minnesota Governor Arne H. Carlson's *Partners for Quality National Governor's Conference*, simply mark the beginning of statewide workshops on Total Quality Education. State Quality Awards for Education in Minnesota, Pennsylvania, Oregon, Florida, and New York State "spotlight" schools engaged in using Total Quality tools and techniques to improve themselves.

The state awards are modeled after the Malcolm Baldridge National Quality Award. The Baldridge award was created by the United States' Department of Commerce in 1987 to encourage and recognize a commitment to quality by U.S. business. It was intended to be similar to Japan's coveted Deming Prize. The interest in the Baldridge award has increased dramatically since its inception, as the requests for applications demonstrate. In 1988, 12,000 companies requested applications; in 1989, 51,000 requests were received. In 1990, the Commerce Department received 180,000 requests. The number of applicants for the Baldridge Prize has gone from 66 in 1988, to 40 in 1989, to 97 applicants in 1990. According to the Application Guidelines, the award is designed to promote:

- ◆ Awareness of quality as an increasingly important element in competitiveness
- ◆ Understanding of the requirements for quality excellence

◆ Sharing of information of successful quality strategies and on the benefits derived from implementation of those strategies.

Applications can be obtained free from the National Institute for Standards and Technology which is part of the United States Department of Commerce. For an application write to:

Malcolm Baldridge National Quality Award
National Institute for Standards and Technology
Administration Building, Room A537
Gaitersburg, MD 20899
Telephone: (301) 975–2036
FAX: (301) 948–3716

The program is designed so that there can be six winners each year (two large manufacturing companies, two large service companies, and two small businesses of either type). All applications are reviewed by 5- or 6-member teams from the Board of Examiners. It is possible to receive 1,000 points on an application. If an application receives a score of 601, the business qualifies for a site visit. During a site visit, examiners spend approximately 3 days touring the facilities, conducting interviews, and reviewing data. Examiners verify information supplied on the written application with their findings made at the site. The findings of the site visit go to Baldridge Award Judges for review. The judges recommend applicants in each category to the National Institute of Standards and Technology. The National Institute of Standards and Technology makes the final recommendation to the United States Secretary of Commerce.

Many companies request and complete applications for the Baldridge Award without the expectation of winning. They simply wish to use the Baldridge criteria to do a self-assessment against specific guidelines. Schools can utilize these criteria in the same manner.

The National Institute of Standards and Technology is studying the feasibility of developing a national award in education. Bills are working their way through Congress establishing an educational component to the Baldridge Award. If an award is developed, it will probably use the Baldridge criteria with some modifications.

Schools interested in investigating criteria for educational excellence might wish to use New York State's Excelsior Award in Education. The Governor's Excelsior Award Program was established in 1991 by Governor Mario M. Cuomo. This program recognizes high quality performance in the private, public, and education sectors. It also provides organizations with a self-assessment tool that enables them to compare themselves to a world-class standard of excellence. A comparison of the two awards (which begins on the next page) shows that the Excelsior Award for Education places a greater emphasis on Leadership and Human Resource Excellence and less importance on Information and Analysis, Strategic Quality Planning, Quality Assurance of Programs and Services, Quality Results, and Client/Customer Satisfaction. Excelsior applications can be obtained free from the New York State Department of Labor. For an application write to:

> The Governor's Excelsior Award
> Barbara Ann Harms, Excelsior Award Administrator
> Governor W. Averell Harriman
> State Office Building Campus
> Building 12 Room 540
> Albany, New York 12240
> (518) 457–6747

The Kenmore-Town of Tonawanda School District, a suburban area of Buffalo, won the Excelsior Award in 1992. The number of schools aligning their processes with local and state awards is increasing. The Eden Prairie School District in Minnesota has been using the Baldridge Criteria as a self-assessment tool.

Growing numbers of schools across the nation are implementing Total Quality Education. (*See* Julie E. Horine's compilation in the October 1993 *Quality Progress* magazine and Betty McCormick's book, *Quality in Education: Critical Linkages* (Princeton Junction, NJ: Eye On Education, 1993).) These schools are generous in sharing their experiences. Many of their efforts are being aided by local and global companies who are using Total Quality Management Techniques to change their businesses.

Comparison of the Malcolm Baldrige Award and the Excelsior Award in Education

Malcolm Baldrige National Quality Award		New York Governor's Excelsior Award—Education	
Categories/Items	Pts.	Categories/Items	Pts.
1.1 Senior Executive Leadership	45	1.1 Senior Executive Leadership	50
1.2 Management for Quality	25	1.2 Management for Quality	30
1.3 Public Responsibility & Corporate Citizenship	25	1.3 Partnering	40
		1.4 Community Responsibility	30
1.0 Leadership—Subtotal	**95**	**1.0 Leadership—Subtotal**	**170**
2.1 Scope & Management of Quality Performance, Data, & Information	15	2.1 Scope & Management of Quality Data & Information	10
2.2 Competitive Comparisons & Benchmarking	20	2.2 Benchmarking & Comparisons	20
2.3 Analyses & Uses of Company-Level Data	40	2.3 Analyses & Uses of Organization-Level Data	20
2.0 Information & Analysis—Subtotal	**75**	**2.0 Information & Analysis—Subtotal**	**50**
3.1 Strategic Quality & Company Performance Planning Process	35	3.1 Strategic Quality & Organizational Performance Planning Process	30

Malcolm Baldridge National Quality Award

Categories/Items	Pts.
3.2 Quality & Performance Plans	25
3.0 Strategic Quality Planning—Subtotal	**60**
4.1 Human Resource Planning & Management	20
4.2 Employee Involvement	40
4.3 Employee Education & Training	40
4.4 Employee Performance & Recognition	25
4.5 Employee Well-Being & Satisfaction	25
4.0 Human Resource Planning & Management—Subtotal	**150**
5.1 Design & Introduction of Quality Products & Services	40

New York Governor's Excelsior Award—Education

Categories/Items	Pts.
3.2 Quality & Performance Plans	20
3.0 Strategic Quality Planning—Subtotal	**50**
4.1 Human Resource Management	30
4.2 Employee Involvement	30
4.3 Education & Training	50
4.4 Employee Performance & Recognition	40
4.5 Employee Well-Being & Morale	30
4.6 Diversity	30
4.7 Employee Partnering	30
4.0 Human Resource Excellence—Subtotal	**240**
5.1 Design/Development & Introduction of Quality Programs & Services	25

Malcolm Baldridge National Quality Award

Categories/Items	Pts.
5.2 Process Management: Product & Service Production & Delivery Processes	35
5.3 Process Management: Business Process & Support Service	30
5.4 Supplier Quality	20
5.0 Management of Process Quality—Subtotal	**140**
6.1 Product & Service Quality Results	70
6.2 Company Operational Results	50
6.3 Business Process & Support Service Results	25
6.4 Supplier Quality Results	35
6.0 Quality & Operational Results	**180**

New York Governor's Excelsior Award—Education

Categories/Items	Pts.
5.2 Process Management—Instructional & Service Processes	20
5.3 Process Management—Administrative Processes & Support Service Quality	20
5.4 Supplier Quality	20
5.5 Quality Assessment	15
5.0 Management of Process Quality—Subtotal	**100**
6.1 Program & Service Quality Results	60
6.2 Operational Results of the Institution	40
6.3 Administrative Process & Support Service Results	25
6.4 Supplier Quality Results	25
6.0 Quality & Operational Results	**150**

Malcolm Baldridge National Quality Award

Categories/Items	Pts.
7.1 Customer Expectations: Current and Future	35
7.2 Customer Relationship Management	65
7.3 Commitment to Customers	15
7.4 Customer Satisfaction Determination	30
7.5 Customer Satisfaction Results	85
7.6 Customer Satisfaction Comparison	70
7.0 Customer Focus & Satisfaction—Subtotal	**300**
TOTAL POINTS	**1000**

New York Governor's Excelsior Award—Education

Categories/Items	Pts.
7.1 Student & Customer Expectations: Current & Future	25
7.2 Student & Customer Relationship Management	55
7.3 Commitment to Students & Customers	15
7.4 Determining Student & Customer Satisfaction	25
7.5 Student & Customer Satisfaction Results	60
7.6 Student & Customer Satisfaction Comparison	60
7.0 Client/Constituent Satisfaction—Subtotal	**240**
TOTAL POINTS	**1000**

Like many, we believe that Total Quality Education must start in elementary school. The American Society for Quality Control's *Koalaty Kid* program is in 60 elementary schools in 17 states, Canada, and Mexico. The program involves parents, community volunteers, teachers, and students in getting elementary school children interested in reading.

Industrialized nations around the world, faced with increased global competition, are demanding educational reform. The following quotation comes from *Enterprise Australia Limited*, November 1991:

> "We are not doing enough, as a nation, to prepare students for the dramatically different workplace they will face in the 21st Century. The next generation must be more creative, more adaptable, more questioning and critical, better able to communicate with others and work together as members of a team, and better equipped to accept and manage change—in other words, to be more enterprising."

A growing number of foreign school systems are utilizing Total Quality to upgrade and restructure their schools. Major efforts are underway in Australia, New Zealand, the former Soviet Union, Ireland, Brazil, Paraguay, and Uruguay. They believe that the Total Quality Education process is replicable. They have witnessed the narrowing of the "Quality Gap" between Japanese manufacturers and American companies. They are aware that "Japanese-made" cars are being manufactured in Tennessee and Ohio.

If we believe that technology alone will save us, America is an endangered nation. America is at a crossroads. We can maintain the current path and get the same results we are now getting or we can change direction—and by using Total Quality Education, we can lead America and the rest of the world into the 21st century. It is our belief at Westinghouse that Total Quality Education will achieve the long-term economic survival of the United States as it competes in the world marketplace.

12

CAN TOTAL QUALITY EDUCATION WORK?

What we are doing in Westinghouse is not an aberration. It can be replicated in other schools and districts. Many schools' efforts, like ours, are in their early, formative, exploratory stages. Total Quality Education has been shown to work not only in Westinghouse but in those schools where it is being implemented. But we should not believe that these limited ventures into Total Quality Education are alone capable of transforming the entire educational system. We must not expect that planting a few seeds of Total Quality Education in individual schools or districts, and expecting them to spread to other schools, will produce a world-class educational system which will properly prepare tomorrow's workforce.

Applying bandaids to a system which is hemorrhaging produces, at best, short-term relief. We must stop tinkering with a system that is failing to satisfy its customers. Too many proposals to change schools tamper with the symptoms of the diseases rather than dealing with the root causes.

We need to raise both the expectations and the achievements of our schools. America cannot maintain a successful global stance without a quality education system. For those traditional schools which are successful, Total Quality Education will only increase their successes. For schools with a high dropout and failure rate, the use of Total Quality Education gives them the ability to transform themselves into world-class schools.

Some groups have proposed passing all students regardless of how much learning has taken place. They feel this will help a student's self-image. Passing everyone helps no one; neither the students who advance to the next grade without the foundation for the material about to be taught nor the society which must cope with ill-prepared workers.

For some the answer is vouchers. Giving parents a check so that they can choose a private school is merely a tax subsidy to the wealthy. Giving parents a check for up to one-fourth of a school bill may permit them to choose a different school, but will, in no way, improve the school they leave.

Many Americans believe that the schools will improve by doing what they have always done—they should just do more of it. Having longer school years and days ignores the fact that students who are not learning now will not benefit from more of the same. Stated differently, if a defective, inefficient automobile was produced in 10 months, how would we increase its performance and reliability if we continued to produce the same automobile in 12 months? The key question is not how long people go to school but what they learn when they are there.

What must be transformed in education, is not the student, the parent, the teacher, or even the curriculum. Rather, we must transform the way the educational system is managed and perceived.

There needs to be a change in the school culture. We must stop accepting the way things are and start doing something about them. American society has built an artificial barrier between schools and the world of work. The barrier must be pulled down collectively by the suppliers and the customers of the school. Transforming education causes the realization that all of the players are on the same side. This team effort will help stop treating each other as adversaries.

TRADITIONAL EDUCATION

TRANSFORMED EDUCATION

Pushing the boulder up the hill becomes easier if we all push in the same direction. In addition, everyone profits when we come together and work for the benefit of the schools.

GOVERNMENT—LOCAL, STATE, AND FEDERAL

Society must reprioritize America's values and raise the status of education and educators. When states or local areas cut their budgets because of poor economic conditions, it is generally education which takes the largest, frequently disproportionate, cut. We must treat education as importantly as we treat highway building, sanitation, and prisons. Education is a vital service! Our nation is being shortsighted when focussing on short-term goals. We are sacrificing the nation's children, schools, and future.

We have to realize the insanity of the current method of funding America's public schools. Inner-city schools, which serve America's poorest children facing the greatest educational challenges, frequently receive the least money. Current funding for education is financed through local property taxes. Voters cast ballots on a general budget which includes corrections, highway building, sanitation, and government salaries. Generally, education and library budgets are separate and voters frequently vent their frustration over high taxes by voting against the education budget because they are unable to identify individual items in the general budget.

Many states use lotteries to provide funding for education. How callous! Imagine if we were to fund government officials' salaries the same way. Expenditures for education must be viewed as a long-term investment. Funding for schools would best be done on a multi-year basis. Long-term planning cannot take place without realistic long-term funding.

We are frequently told that education is expensive. It isn't. It is the lack of education which is expensive. It is expensive to the individual who cannot get a job in America. It is expensive to the society which doesn't get another technologically trained member of the workforce. Yet educational spending in our cities, in real dollars, has decreased. According to the *New York Times* (October 30, 1993:27), ". . .[W]hen inflation is taken into account the city [New York] is spending about 8 percent less per student than it did in 1990."

Everybody talks about the costs and failures in education but not of prison spending. "In the fiscal year 1992, states spent more than $15 billion operating prison systems and more than $2 billion building prisons. The growth in operating costs is expected to increase, on average, by about 5 percent in the current fiscal year, but spending on construction is expected to double, to about $4 billion as 112 new prisons are opened to house 75,000 more inmates." (*New York Times*, August 7, 1992.) There always seems to be enough money for our prisons.

In 1990, a year at Rikers Island (a prison in New York City) cost $52,496 per year per inmate. A year in the New York City public schools cost $6,439. Median family income was $35,225. (Howard Kurtz, "New York, Jail City," *New York Magazine*, April 23, 1990:39–44.)

"'The way we're addressing the problem is absurd. This is about people who can't read, can't write, are addicted to drugs, can't get a job, and they hurt other people,' stated Richard Koehler, former New York City Corrections Commissioner. 'More than 60 percent of city inmates read below the sixth-grade level and could be classified as functionally illiterate.'" (Howard Kurtz, "New York, Jail City," *New York Magazine*, April 23, 1990:39–44.)

Richard Wade, Professor of History at the Graduate Center of the City University of New York, stated:

> The cost of illiteracy is up to $200 billion annually, if we take into account unemployment, health, welfare, and incarceration. New York State's bill alone is about $20 billion, in large part the result of an overburdened criminal justice system. Each inmate costs the State $150 a day, more than $50,000 per year. By every estimate, the majority of the 60,000 prisoners in New York State and the 21,000 in New York City are functionally illiterate. They enter illiterate, leave illiterate, and, more often than not, return illiterate. . . .
>
> More than 40 percent returned to jail within three years, and 20 percent more within five years. In Japan, by contrast, convicts cannot get out of prison until they

can read and write. The recidivism rate there is 5 percent.

Thomas A. Coughlin 3rd, New York State Corrections Commissioner, estimates that the United States spends $20 billion annually on its prison system. (*New York Times,* July 7, 1992.) Others, including Governor Wilder of Virginia, place the cost as high as $25 billion.

The recidivism rate in prisons has been estimated as high as 80% over a 5-year period. In many cities our prisons are air conditioned, but not our schools. Our prisons have cable TV, but not many of our schools! Is this the message we wish to send to our young people?

We must start paying teachers more. By not paying teachers higher salaries we are discouraging entry into teaching. Schools have difficulty finding people qualified to teach many subjects, including computer literacy, because many college graduates choose to enter the workplace where salaries are higher and working conditions better. Rather than raising teacher salaries in order to attract better qualified people, we lower our standards. Many science and math teachers have had little or no college-level math or science.

If someone were to tell a parent that their child was dying, cost would not be a factor in finding the best doctor. Yet, we are not willing to pay our teachers well and our children's future is dying. By limiting teacher salaries, we are limiting America's capacity to produce the best scientists, doctors, and engineers.

"Our society cries out desperately for major investment in many areas. But investment in our young people should be our highest priority. . . . [Today] . . . many urban youngsters approach school totally unprepared and face the difficult, if not impossible task, of 'catching up'. School buildings are dilapidated, detrimental to the learning process, and not up to the technological standards required. . . . And finally, while teachers and principals are as caring as ever, frustration, poor pay, and cuts in professional and leadership training budgets have taken their toll." (Ruben Mark, Chairman, President, and C.E.O. of Colgate-Palmolive Co., *New York Times,* July 7, 1992.)

Additional funding for our schools could come from the federal government or from state or local education-dedicated sales taxes, similar to one which recently passed in the city of San Francisco.

These changes should take place, like Total Quality in Education, over a period of time. The Department of Education can, with State Departments of Education design a strategic plan for implementation.

We must not believe that money alone will solve the ills of education. Those who support the need for education must become more vocal and proactive with our government officials and policymakers. If schools continue to have dropouts, then the country will become less productive; the tax base falters and shrinks; other industrialized nation's products become more desirable. There has to be recognition of this theorem.

THE BUSINESS COMMUNITY

We must get more businesspeople demanding and encouraging change in the schools. The largest customer of the schools is the business community. Not only does supporting change in our schools make moral sense, it makes economic sense.

The business community, by placing a value on grades and attendance and success in school, can send a message to students, parents, and the school community that those areas are important. Business could require that student applicants submit grade and attendance records when they apply for part-time or entry-level employment. Applicants with superior grades and attendance records could receive hiring priority. Graduates with low absences and tardies could be recognized in some manner.

PARENTS

Parents must be actively involved in helping children to learn. Those who can afford to should volunteer their time and lobby state and local governments for programs which help the schools. They should demonstrate to their children, by example, that education is important. They should be going to their

Parents Teachers Association and Board of Education meetings and attending Open School Nights.

SCHOOLS

ADMINISTRATION

Teaching Total Quality Education techniques and tools must begin in the early grades. Waiting until high school is too late. The American Society for Quality Control's *Koalaty Kid* program has demonstrated the success of having Total Quality reaching into the early grades. The success of other programs which work can no longer be ignored. Research has shown that for every dollar invested into programs like "Head Start," society saves $6 on dropout prevention.

Teaching is an art. Professional educators make it look simple. Their primary role is aiding in the transmission of knowledge. Teacher talents include: being a friend, counselor, tutor, coach, role-model, and, increasingly, surrogate parenting. They must not only assist in the transmission of knowledge, but must teach values, driving skills, sex education, and swimming and collect money for book sales. Many people think that a teacher is only working when he or she is standing in front of classroom full of students. Few understand the hours of preparation that go into developing lesson plans, developing and marking of tests, preparing grades, or calling parents.

Little time is devoted to ongoing staff development. Teachers in a school are frequently unable to learn new techniques or how to deal with disruptive students who do not wish to be in a classroom. When we offer incentives to teachers to take in-service training, frequently this training is taken by individuals seeking incentive pay. Senior teachers are not required to take additional training. Group in-service training frequently doesn't exist.

We demand that doctors and airline pilots know the latest developments in their field. We give them on-the-job training. But when it comes to training senior teachers, we seemingly cannot afford to have time taken away from classroom instruction. State governments must permit schools to set aside noninstructional days for training and provide funding for the training. Administrators and supervisors should petition school boards for meaningful staff development in Total Quality techniques.

EDUCATORS

Educators must take an active role in seeking a transformation in the schools. Just as educators have changed since they began teaching, so have the schools. Teachers must come to realize that education should be student-centered, just as businesses should be customer-centered. They should ask, "How did what happened in class today further the students' knowledge and add to their life's experiences?"

Educators should be developing and revising curriculum utilizing Total Quality techniques and applying the tools in the classroom.

There should be a realization that educators can aid their suppliers. High schools should be aiding middle schools. Middle schools should be assisting elementary schools. Lines of communication should be developed so that teachers and administrators at one educational level can discuss the strengths and weaknesses of students who progress to the next educational level. High school students can tutor younger students as can middle school students.

COLLEGES AND UNIVERSITIES

Those in higher education can assist their suppliers. They can supply tutors and mentors. They can provide additional resources to the public schools. An empty seat in a college class or laboratory doesn't cost anything extra if it is filled by an interested high school or middle school student.

Preparing potential teachers and administrators in Schools of Education with Total Quality techniques makes just as much sense as preparing business majors with the same techniques.

Many college and university instructors whose job it is to prepare potential teachers and administrators have not been in the public schools. A requirement for teaching potential teachers should be an awareness of what is happening in our nation's public schools.

What will America look like in the 21st century? Schools that do well in the next century will have to be "smart schools." That is, schools which provide the means for students to learn on their own, teachers who serve as facilitators, principals and superintendents who provide their customers with the means to succeed.

Lester Thurow, in *Head to Head: The Coming Economic Battle Among Japan, Europe, and America* (New York, 1993:299), wrote:

> "We and our children will not have a world-class standard of living, and some of the chances for the good things in life that Americans have come to expect . . . will diminish. Not doing anything is far worse than doing something."

Whatever we choose to do about the future, we must come to the realization that our vision is dependent on our transformation of the school system. Someone once said, "If we continue to do what we have always been doing we will continue to get what we have always been getting." America can no longer afford having the schools give us the same results. Total Quality Education has demonstrated that it can change the results.

This chapter will be interpreted by some as an excuse not to begin the transformation immediately. As has been stated throughout this book, America's schools cannot continue to do what they have been doing. The perpetuation of a failed process will only result in continued failure.

Some educators will insist that they cannot make changes without additional funding from the federal, state, or local government. We the educators must begin the process in our classrooms, our schools, and our districts. Waiting for the cavalry to ride in and rescue the schools simply means accepting the status quo.

We have the power to change things! Do we have the desire to do so?

Appendix A

GEORGE WESTINGHOUSE'S VOCATIONAL COURSES

The following vocational courses are offered at George Westinghouse Vocational and Technical High School:

BUSINESS MACHINE MAINTENANCE & REPAIR

By the time a student has completed this course, he or she is proficient with all the "tools of the trade" needed in troubleshooting repair procedures, adjustment and servicing techniques on all forms of typewriters, duplicating machines, word processors and computers. Students also gain an understanding of multimeter functions, schematics, and their applications.

CABINETMAKING & WOODWORKING

By the time a student has completed the Woodworking Program, he or she is already experienced in actual furniture making, advanced machine operation, and renovation construction. Graduates who have studied renovation construction have had on-the-job training under union supervision. All students are versed in construction theory.

COMPUTER PROGRAMMING & APPLICATIONS

Students who have graduated this 3-year course are knowledgeable in advanced PASCAL, as well as COBOL, Advanced BASIC, BASIC-PLUS, and other languages. Using Tandy 1000's (capable of running all major business software), as well as TRS-80 models II, III and IV, and the DEC 11/34, students learn rogramming and the use of applications software including spreadsheet, database, and word processing.

COMPUTER TECHNOLOGY

Graduates of this course are students from the Technical Electronics program who have chosen to specialize in computers. A knowledge of digital electronics, computer mechanics, electromagnetic devices, microprocessors, and peripherals prepares graduates for employment in any company involved with computers. They are skilled at computer troubleshooting and maintenance.

DENTAL LABORATORY PROCESSING TECHNICIAN

A student graduating this course is familiar with copper plating dies, self-articulation models, wax up inlays, splints and bridgework soldering, and porcelain jacket crowns. He or she has learned to create plaster and stone models of uppers and lowers, palate acrylic trays, and comprehensive denture work.

ELECTRICAL INSTALLATION & PRACTICE

A graduate of this program is qualified to work on residential and industrial installations, including basic trade lighting and low voltage signal circuits (bell wiring, telephones, and burglar and fire alarm systems). He or she is knowledgeable in design and theory of wiring and has worked either in actual renovation construction under union supervision, or motor control and motor wiring.

ELECTRO-MECHANICAL DRAFTING & FINE LINE DRAWING

Graduates of this course are already fully qualified as drafters with experience in cooperative work programs through the senior year. Working on a basis of mechanical drafting, they have learned the basics of computer-aided drafting (CAD), machine drafting, geometrics, developments, electrical, architectural, and structural drawing.

ELECTRONIC OCCUPATIONS

Graduates of this course are proficient in the use of electronic tools and equipment, including digital multimeters, oscilloscopes, signal generators, analog multimeters, and electronic trainers. They are trained in digital electronics in computers, as well as amplifiers, power supplies, and other applications of electronic theory.

JEWELRY MAKING

A student finishing this course has learned jewelry design, wax and rubber model making, rendering, toolmaking, electroplating, and other techniques. He or she has performed stone-setting, metal enameling, machine and hand engraving, and has been trained in the use of jewelers' saws, needle hand files, and other tools.

OPTICAL MECHANICS TECHNICIAN

Graduates of this course have experience in surfacing plastic and glass lenses, including bifocals, cylinder generator operation, beveling, and related benchwork. They have worked on eyeglass frame patternmaking, decentration and refraction of lenses, and inserting lenses in all shapes of eyeglass frames.

Westinghouse is the only high school in the United States with an optical mechanics technical program.

TECHNICAL ELECTRONICS

Graduates of this program are knowledgeable in digital and medical electronics and have conducted experiments with transistors and other solid state devices. The course includes building electronic amplifiers and working on electronic drafting, transformers, diodes, and LED's. In addition to the technical areas, students are required to take a full Regents academic program.

TELEVISION STUDIO TECHNOLOGY

Students in this course of study are trained in the operation, installation, and testing of video and audio equipment, including broadcasting and cable TV. The course features instruction in photographic lighting, special effects, and other areas. The Studio Technology course is a specialized study for students who have already taken the general Technical Electronic course. Upon graduation, students are eligible for the FCC license exam.

Appendix B

CONTACTS

ORGANIZATIONS

American Association of School Administrators (A.A.S.A.)
1801 North Moore Street,
Arlington VA 22209–9988
 (703) 875–0753

American Society for Quality Control, Inc. (A.S.Q.C.)
611 East Wisconsin Avenue,
P.O. Box 3005
Milwaukee, WI 53201–3005

GOAL/QPC
13 Branch Street
Methuen, MA 01844
(508) 685–3900

National Educational Quality Initiative (N.E.Q.I.)
Dr. Ronald L. Heilmann, President
1819 S. Green Bay Road
Grafton, WI 53201
(414) 229–6259

MAGAZINES

Quality Digest (published monthly)
QCI International
1350 Vista Way
Red Bluff, CA 96080

Quality Progress (published monthly)
American Society for Quality Control, Inc.
611 East Wisconsin Avenue
P.O. Box 3005
Milwaukee, WI 53201–3005

NEWSLETTERS

Creating Quality K-12 (published monthly)
Magna Publications, Inc.
2718 Dryden Drive
 Madison, WI 53704–3086
(800) 433–0499

Critical Linkages II Newsletter
Sager Educational Enterprises
Dr. Carol Sager
Sager Educational Enterprises
21 Wallis Road
Chesnut Hill, MA 02167
(617) 469–9644

Quality Network News (published bi-monthly)
American Association of School Administrators
1801 North Moore Street
Arlington VA 22209–9988
(703) 875–0753

Total Quality and Site-Based Management Journal
(published bi-monthly)
National Center to Save Our Schools
Kay Rizzuto
P.O. Box 948
Westbury, NY 11590
(516) 997–1777/9555

Appendix C

BIBLIOGRAPHY

The number of books appearing about Total Quality Management and Total Quality Education is growing exponentially. In order to assist the reader who may have limited time constraints the author has arranged books he has used by topics. The books which have been found the most helpful are in **bold print**.

EDUCATION

American Association of School Administrators (AASA) *Creating Quality Schools,* 1992.

A Nation at Risk: The Imperative for Educations Reform, the National Commission on Execellence in Education, commissioned by T.H. Bell, Secretary of Education, issued April 1983.

U.S. Department of Education. *America 2000: A Sourcebook,* 1991.

Bonstingl, John J. *Schools of Quality: An Introduction to TQM in Education.* The Association for Supervision and Curriculum Development (ASCD), 1992.

Brumberg, Stephan F. *Going to America Going to School,* Praeger, 1986.

Byrnes, Margaret A., Cornesky, Robert A., & Byrnes, Lawrence W. *The Quality Teacher*. Cornesky & Associates, 1992.

Cotter, Maury & Seymour, Daniel. *Kidgets*. American Society for Quality Control Press, 1993.

Fiske, Edward B. *Smart Schools, Smart Kids*. Simon and Shuster, 1991.

Glasser, William M. *The Quality School*, Perennial Library, Harper and Row, 1990.

Glasser, William M. *The Quality School Teacher: A Companion Volume to the Quality School*. Perennial Library, Harper and Row, 1993.

Harris, John W., & Baggett, J. Mark. *Quality Quest in the Academic Process*. Samford University, 1992.

Kazuo, Ishizaka. *School Education in Japan*. International Society for International Information, Inc., 1978.

Kearns, David T., & Doyle, Denis P. *Winning the Brain Race: A Bold Plan to Make Our Schools Competitive*. Institute for Contemporary Studies, 1989.

Kozol, Jonathan. *Savage Inequalities: Children in America's Schools*. Crown Publishers, 1991.

McCormick, Betty L. *Quality & Education: Critical Linkages*. Eye on Education, 1993.

National Alliance of Business. *The Cutting Edge of Common Sense, Using Total Quality to Reinvent Education*, 1992.

EMPOWERMENT

Belasco, James A. *Teaching the Elephant How to Dance: The Manager's Guide to Empowering Change*. Plume Book, 1990.

Byham, William C., & Cox, Jeff. *Zapp!* New York, 1988.

INDUSTRY

Barker, Joel Arthur. *Future Edge: Discovering the New Paradigms of Success*. William Morrow & Co., 1992.

Boyett, Joseph H., & Conn, Henry P. *Workplace 2000*. Plume, 1991.

Glasser, William M. *The Control Theory Manager*. Harper Perennial, 1994.

Halberstram, David. *The Reckoning*. Avon Books, 1986.

Kolberg, William H., & Smith, Foster C. *Rebuilding America's Workforce*. Business One Irwin, 1992.

Noble, Sara P. *301 Great Management Ideas*. Goldhirsh Group, 1991.

Peters, Tom, & Waterman, Jr., Robert H. *In Search of Excellence*. Warner Books, 1982.

Peters, Tom & Austin, Nancy. *A Passion For Excellence*. Warner Books, 1985.

Reich, Robert B. *Tales of A New America*. Times Books, 1987.

Riley, Pat. *The Winner Within: A Life Plan for Team Players*. G.P. Putnam's Sons, 1993.

Research Alert. *Future Vison: The 189 Most Important Trends of the 1990's*. Sourceooks Trade, 1991.

Senge, Peter M. *The Fifth Discipline: The Art & Practice of The Learning Organization*. Currency Book, 1990.

Thurow, Lester. *Head to Head: The Coming Battle Among Japan, Europe, and America*. Warner Books, 1992.

LEADERSHIP

Covey, Stephen R. *The 7 Habits of Highly Effective People*.

Covey, Stephen R. *Principle-Centered Leadership*. Summit Books, 1990.

DePree, Max. *Leadership is an Art*. Dell Trade Paperback, 1989.

Juran, J.M. *Juran on Leadership for Quality: An Exceutive Handbook*. The Free Press, 1989.

TOTAL QUALITY MANAGEMENT

Aguayo, Rafael. *Dr. Deming The American Who Taught the Japanese about Quality*. Simon & Shuster, 1990.

Albrecht, Karl, & Zemke, Ron. *Service America: Doing Business in the New Economy*. Dow Jones-Irwin, 1985.

Blanchard, Ken, & Bowles, Sheldon. *Raving Fan: A Revolutionary Approach to Customer Service*. William Morrow & Company, 1993.

Bowles, Jerry, & Hammond, Joshua. *Beyond Quality: New Standards of Total Performance Than Can Change the Future of Corporate America*. Berkley Books, 1991.

Crawford-Mason, Clare, and Dobbyns, Lloyd. *Thinking About Quality: Progress, Wisdon, and the Deming Philosophy.* Times Books, 1994.

Crosby, Philip B. *Quality is Free: The Art of Making Quality Certain.* Mentor, 1979.

Crosby, Philip B. *Running Things The Art of Making Things Happen.* Mentor Books, 1986.

Crosby, Philip B. *The Eternally Successful Organization.* Penguin Books, 1988.

Capezio, Peter, & Morehouse, Debra. *Taking the Mystery Out of TQM.* Career Press, 1993.

Deming, W. Edwards. *Quality, Productivity and Competitive Position.* Massachusetts Institute of Technology, 1982.

Deming, W. Edwards. *Out of the Crisis.* Massachusetts Institute of Technology, 1982.

Dobyns, Lloyd, & Crawford-Mason, Clare. *Quality or Else: The Revolution in World Business.* Houghton Mifflin, 1991.

Gabor, Andrea. *The Man Who Discovered Quality.* Times Books, 1990.

Glasser, William M. *The Control Theory Manager.* Harper Perennial, 1994.

Halberstram, David. *The Reckoning.* Avon Books, 1986.

Hunt, V. Daniel. *Quality in America: How to Implement a Competitive Quality Program.* Business One Irwin, 1992.

Ishikawa, Kaoru. *What is Total Quality Control?: The Japanese Way.* Prentice Hall, 1985.

Juran, J.M. *Juran on Planning For Quality.* The Free Press, 1988.

Kearns, David T., & Doyle, Denis P. *Winning the Brain Race: A Bold Plan to Make Our Schools Competitive.* Institute for Contemporary Studies, 1989.

Scherkenback, William W. *Deming's Road to Continual Improvement.* SPC Press, 1991.

Scholtes, Peter R. *The Team Handbook.* Joiner Associates, 1988.

Schonberger, Richard J. *Japanese Manufacturing Techniques: Nine Hidden Lessons in Simplicity.* The Free Press, 1982.

Smith, Steve, & Smalley, Mark. *Total Quality: Best Practice in The USA and Japan.* PA Quality Management Services, 1987.

Townsend, Patrick L., & Gebhardt, Joan E. *Quality in Action: 93 Lessons in Leadership, Participation, and Measurement.* John Wiley and Sons, Inc., 1992.

Tribus, Myron. *Quality First: Selected Papers on Quality & Productivity Improvement*. National Institute for Engineering Managment & Systems, 1992.

Walton, Mary. *Deming Management at Work*. G.P. Putnam's Sons, 1990.

Walton, Mary. *The Deming Management Method*. Perigee Books, 1986.

Whiteley, Richard C. *The Customer Driven Company: Moving From Talk to Action*. Addison-Wesley Publishing, 1991.

TOOLS

AT&T. *Process Quality Management & Improvement Guidelines*, 1987.

Digital Equipment Corporation. *Teamwork Tools*.

GOAL/QPC. *The Memory Jogger for Education*, 1992.

Juran Institute. *Quality Improvement Guide*, 1993.

Scherkenback, William W. *The Deming Route to Quality and Productivity: Road Maps and Roadblocks*. Ceep Press, 1986.

VIDEOS

American Society for Quality Control and American Association for School Administrators. *Continuous Quality Improvement: A New Look for Education*.

Crawford-Mason, Claire. *Quality in Education—Deming in the Schools*.

Goal/QPC. *Total Quality Management in Education*.